As Long as You're Breathing

Cristina Firtala

Introduction

As Long As You're breathing is a collection of poetry centred around the concept of oxygen ruling us- of course metaphorically, to express the power and profundity of our human experience, when we seize control over our body, mind and heart. It captures elements of love, existence and purpose through self-evaluation and perspective.

To want and need

We break fine lines between what we need and what we want.
We misinterpret our humanity for artificial supremacy but in reality, we aren't even in
control of our own humanity.
Let's eradicate emotion and implement devotion right, a devotion to a world deserted of life?
It's like we've discovered an entire island but choose to live at the bottom of the ocean.
Dream big, let go.
Build mountains of your emotions only to climb to the top and forget your way down, because this world doesn't teach you to let go, only to dream big and build bigger.
We accelerate our lives on a speed limit to succeed.
But our runways are built to not only set you, but a plane free too.
You need to walk, to experience, even if your back aches and heart breaks
only a life's walk can fix those mistakes.
You don't need a car to pass the motorway of your pain,
or fly a plane just to stay sane so you can be above the splinters of everything you tore apart.
You don't need anything external to fill your heart, internal is an earth full.
I know you like the quicker, the artificial way out,
but your heart is too full of life to ever feel at drought.
So, forget the escape and indulge in the ache,

because one day you'll be forced on that plane wishing you could jump into all the splinters of the worlds love but, the exits are locked and your too far to even see what love looks like in- reality.

Welcome to your reminder.

For the fire that burnt in your soul,
for the fireworks that ignite your emotions,
for the rain that drowns your thoughts into a puddle,
I wanted to say that you are lucky.
You are lucky to have something that burns in your soul -a
reminder that you are alive, that you can be burned yet kept
warm by the same entity.
You are lucky to have fireworks that gather crowds of love and
set off into a beautiful imagery across the sky of your soul,
a reminder that a minor burst of joy even if it is short lived, can
fill your heart and never leave you empty.
You are lucky to have the weight of raindrops fall upon a naked
thought, to feel something other than your words tiptoe on
your mind,
to feel as if the universe is still by your side after all the
umbrellas you placed upon your head,
 when all rain wanted to do was to save you.
You are lucky to be alive, a reminder in itself that when you
awake
your greatest dream will be your greatest life,
as long as you are breathing you have the strength of the
universe.
Realise this, you are lucky.

You are alive.

Purpose is yours

I don't want to lose tomorrow to superficial laughter,
or sightless eyes for the meaningful,
 I'd rather let myself fall into an unknown ground,
maybe there I'd feel safe and sound,
but also proud of the depth- I could have found.
 I don't want to lose tomorrow to the life of obligation;
 to work to avoid starvation,
to feel drained just to sustain,
to fight just to see light.
I don't want to lose tomorrow to someone else's purpose,
just so I can breathe amongst the ones I stole fulfilment from,
while I'm given work to pay my stay,
something someone else worked and prayed for, for years,
just because I couldn't face my fears.
I don't want to lose tomorrow to sightless eyes that can't see
that the image of life is broken and damaged,
while I can't restore the image to look whole again.
But I can't do this because the image isn't modified, my view is.
The only one who can see it whole is the one it belongs to.
I don't want to lose tomorrow to a life that isn't mine,
because my life feels whole even before I could touch it.
I'm going to take my life back- today.

Dear you,

You may feel like surrendering is a way out,
but what if death isn't an escape?
When your eyes close for what you hope to be the last time,
you imagine this pain dissolving as you lose life or magically
flushing out of existence but maybe- just maybe, it won't.
Have you ever imagined that maybe death is the imprisonment
and life is freedom?
When you die, you don't lose the pain but are stuck with it
forever, there is no tomorrow to feel better,
 there is nothing ever but that pain that's imbedded into the
material of your soul, imbedded and not drawn.
Permanent not washable.
 I know that right now you feel like the pain is imbedding into
you already,
 but whilst you're breathing the pain can only be drawn, as long
as you are breathing you have the freedom to find an eraser.
 Yes, life is temporary,
but the drawings of temporary happiness have the most
everlasting effects,
you are able to modify and erase a mistake,
it slowly creates a beautiful masterpiece.
Death will never even give you a pencil.

Dear you,

I promise life is your answer- death is your question,
questioning your
emptiness until you wish for life.
 So, don't give up,
you're powerful.

Self-conscious?

You are a queen.
A queen?
No.
You reign more than his kingdom.
A Goddess?
Perhaps, but you are not to be defined,
even by honey drizzled words or the synonyms of poignant
fragrances.
Your name shall be found in the midst of painting the Mona
Lisa and the beginning of a new existence, the revolution of
you.
Where souls dream, light dances and the senses coordinate,
you ~~are~~ belong in the magic of beauty and enchanted thoughts.
Maybe you've forgotten,
but your body is not a castle.
Your mind is not a sample,
and your heart is not a waterfall.
Your body is revolutionary artwork, virtual to all yet visual to
those who understand the technology of you.
Your mind is the encyclopaedia of a life full of good fortune one
you cannot share with those convicted of stealing will power.
Of course, your heart.
Waterfall, this is your image.
You are built with unlimited love to pour like a waterfall,
But the location is not unlimited in movement, rather-
immobile.
Choose with enchanted thoughts where to place yours.
Who are you?
Are you self-conscious?
You choose everything you wish to be,
a castle, a sample a waterfall,

or,
unlimited and undefinable.

Old and new

Happiness was never about the new life,
 or when you aim to accomplish something.
It's your room décor, you have everything you need to decorate,
to complete.
You just need to find the right colour combination, the right
arrangement with everything you already have.

Suicide

If you left right now,
the movie will end but,
you're not the only actor in it or audience watching it,
or the only one living from this movie.
If you left,
The entire cast would lose their place,
because you didn't realise this was a series filled with
everything you've ever wanted.
If you left all the epic scripted words, all the unforgettable
improvised scenes, all the fans and all the adventure would
burn in the flames of your- regret.
Before you think about leaving think about your way there.
The stars you could name, to feel the love of all continuums,
dreams you could restore, lives you'll save,
and watching the one thing you thought you'll never have dive
into your arms.
You're not the only actor,
turn around,
there is an entire auditorium watching,
because you are the hero in this film,
with the role to save,
save yourself.

Save yourself.
            Give life another chance.

A letter to emotion.

I cannot encapsulate all the aches of the world into a poem, or a
book, but here's a list
of some things you may need to hear.

To anger,
You have a sweet tooth for catastrophe, but you forget that
sugar dissolves in water. Fill yourself with enough resistance
and joy, for the anger to feel like a single
crystal of sugar- amongst the body of happiness.

To regret,
 I know you weigh about the same as the universe compacted
within a mind and heart, but everything floats in space, look at
it this way, the weight of the ache will never
change but how and where it survives does. Make your mind a
place of acceptance, understanding and peace and maybe, just
maybe regret will no longer feel heavy, as it begins to float.

To love,
You are oxygen. Some people intoxicate you and so they choose
to breathe the idea of
you into toxicity, but alone you are clean, reliable and
everlasting in your lifetime.
If it is clean love, they will never leave your side, they will fight
for you, protect you, compromise, treasure and respect your
needs. They will build with you until the day they run out of

oxygen, because love holds the same commitment as oxygen does to
you.

To anxiety,
I know it feels like within seconds you're going to completely dismantle, your instruction manual to survival is torn and you have seconds to find the way out. Breathe and listen, your survival manual was designed by you, you know how to escape because this imprisonment is your creation, breathe and look around this is where you've built yourself, and it is where you'll always piece yourself together. You
are safe, fear will pass, and everything will fall into place.

To sadness,
You are like a drop of food colouring into perfectly clean water, you make it harder for
it to serve its purpose. But as you fight through the sadness, realise that holding the strength to keep hope in your eyes will help you turn this puddle of stained sadness into a clean happiness. You are strong enough to cleanse.

Brutality doesn't fix.

Occasionally we sew worn clothing back together once its completely fallen apart because we treasure the memories that's making it so cotton soft.
We use a razor-sharp needle and an attenuated thread- yet we still question why it falls apart again.

A spilt bucket of depression

When a bucket fills, a caution sign spills
A masquerade of violet valour yet packaged with a
deoxygenated smile,
some days I'd watch eyes performing a pirouette as the mop
engaged but never voluntarily
Other days, I was the paralysed authoritarian imploring the
mop to absorb my spilt tribulation.
You see the cuts, the open wounds of the bucket
We see the spillage, the mess
Only I can see the blade that cut it
Again, and again I watched, litres after litres poured into the
bucket all of which was designed to clean my spilt pain
Magical elixirs formed in the laboratory of my imagination
Litres after litres wasted and frustrated but litres are not feather
weight
This psychological litre of mess deteriorates you, expecting the
bucket to unveil no stains, no marks
and if the curtains split like the divorce of hope from my life
and the buckets blood begins to drip, will it be enough to say I
only bled to cover up the cracks or will I
still be irreparable to you?
Now that my cuts show like an abstract piece of art in a gallery,
why does the artwork
receive an applause and I a caution sign?

This blade isn't known to the human eye, it's not one of sharp edges or slicing margins. So hit pause on observing life with just eyes.

Exit this illusion

Search for the blade with emotion, empathy and sympathy.

A blade has an edge, an end

It has a margin, an escape

It has a handle to hold and release, here you decide if it's worth your peace,

When you find this blade remember why we are told to be careful with scissors

Did you find it yet? If not, here it is.

Your suicidal thoughts.

Do not crack your bucket because with or without a mark a bucket's purpose will always remain, it will always be able to be filled again.

Live unmarked, untouched and maybe then you'll receive the applause of an abstract piece of art for the life you've filled and not spilled, while you place featherweight

beauty in the place of litres of depression's waste.

Mathematical errors to life

We look for answers in expressions
and assume equations have no answers.

Oxygen

"why do you take back oxygen even though it keeps leaving you?"

But it doesn't leave you.
It's never left you.
You long for the emotion parallel to full oxygenated lungs.
So of course, you will confuse them for oxygen,
when visually those two parallel lines seem identically in love.
Identically distant,
where the distance oxygen took from you breathed them in so
intoxicated in order for you to understand, they are the waste
product of our existence.
You see oxygen will never leave you, the waste product of
respiration does; and although air and oxygen, them and
survival look identical,
the particles that compose this emotion have never even met.
They have no intention of meeting you and its parallel love.
 So, don't wait until the day you and oxygen can become best
friends and stop this war, because that'll be the day in which
you will need to stop utilizing its beauty and forcing it to
surrender to your cruel intent.
The day oxygen can live its own life without your inhalation.
Your destruction, because that day will be the day oxygen will
hand you two glasses,
one with a lid and one without.
You'll have to choose one.

You will think they are parallel, visually identical, but the one with a lid keeps oxygen imprisoned so tell me, is being imprisoned better than being free but lost of your identity? Remember the day oxygen leaves your inhalation into an exhalation it is no longer oxygen.

If you don't walk away now, the day you somehow will, it's no longer you.

Choose between your breaths.

Will you walk away from them now or will you wait until the day oxygen

decides to leave you,
because the day oxygen leaves you- they will breathe?

My note,

You burned the damage within you, without setting the love on
fire.
because you understood the difference between what is truly
good for you and what appears to be.
You dropped the boulders of your anxieties when you saw
pebbles,
because you realised worrying about things you cannot control,
allows a healthy heart to deal with just the worries in your
palms.
You found your peace and instead of planning out the future,
you completely melted into that moment of happiness.
because you've experienced that pure happiness is like glitter in
sand.
And sometimes you think the world could blend you with pain
and crush you alive, and you'll somehow became whole the
minute he touches you, because he is the magic you discover in
fairy-tales.

You are not.

You are not anything that begins with words.

Lost or found,
with eyes upon a hurricane of hatred,
nor in purgatory between limits and definitions,
between possibility and statistics.

You are not anything that ends with people.

Those whom you begin with or find,
like learning the language of dependency,
you will not use every word, every day.
You are not to be found,
not to be discovered,
but to breathe as a whisper, tinting and staining in your silence.
What does it say?

I- almost understood.

The strength of a woman

You could never staple a woman's elegance onto an instruction manual, because you could never leave fingerprints on her mind and erase the part where, she'll never forget how easily paper can tear.

Independence

The only thing that will heal you,
is realising that you are alone.
A human surrounded by holograms,
soft skin but hearts of stone,
when you need and need the most you need to understand that
you live in a virtual reality.
Because no one will ever be there every time you are in need.
Although people are tangible at skin's depth, they are illusions
to a soul that needs.
It is truly like our needs are poison, and perhaps they are,
 they need to be reacted and dissolved, but no one will touch
your poison if their hands are medicine.
We live like encyclopaedias of wonder but our needs poison
every chance of the life we need.
And maybe we are made to be alone, yes surrounded but alone
at our souls' core,
because when we realise that we are alone, the only need that is
surviving, is the need to heal our self.

Today or tomorrow

Possibly once in your life, maybe twice,
you went somewhere with no idea in your mind of what could
have awaited you.
Maybe a late drive unaware of the time and you caught the
sunset.
Or visiting a new store and finding your dream jewellery piece.
You walked in empty and left full.
The next day you expect to go back at roughly the same time
and catch the sunset again, or maybe you didn't have enough
money yesterday so you're hoping to buy it today.
But the sun doesn't set at that time and the jewellery is out of
stock.
You walked in full and left, completely empty.
Don't sacrifice today's joy, for tomorrow's uncertainty.

Ageing

We all discover the same world in different nuances.
Children in vibrant colours, energetic and full of adventure,
teenagers through a spectrum of light, a frequency of light and
dark, and
of course, adulthood a stage too busy and overflowing to even
see colour,
but if we do pastels are our view.
Time loves what it does so dearly and freely and their age is its
offspring,
 without ever realising that we raise it until time dissolves us,
and everything in between.

My triune

People like to make assumptions based upon view.
A smile is not happiness.
Money isn't health.
The offering of one's hand is not always kindness.
Call it good and evil, call it what religion does- nothing is ever
going to fix a cracked
world.
The secret is- in order to do more than just survive you need to
learn acceptance. Understand that there is pain in all that
grows to be beautiful.
Strength to cry and scream but know exactly when to say you
are ready to carry on
pushing.
And finally, you need intensity.
Something- anything that awakens your soul enough so that
giving up wouldn't be
an option- because you'd lose the chance to feel it again.

Sacrifice

Do you accept?
That some of your hopes will never resurrect.
And your favourite memories will never intercept
this happiness, that today you may or may not have felt.
Your world could be a monument, but if it's locked in your
house,
it's safe,
from harm, but also from fame.
Do you accept?
That some of your moments will never lay in ice,
but heat will dissolve them into pictures and flames, that if you
do not set them free, they may or, may never suffice.
For passion, you must sacrifice.

Measures of beauty?

Beauty has no connection to size.
A cherry blossom tree has beauty beyond infinity.
But a butterfly also fills hearts with irreplaceable serenity.

To expose or cover the world

What if there was such a thing as colour coded charisma?
People wearing emotions in all colours of the rainbow, would
that help you help people, or help you stay away- better?
Maybe the facades of I'm fine, smiles and all the pain that can
define are as fragile as porcelain, yet colour can break through
and let emotion shine.
If we wore our emotions like we wear our eyes on our face and
skin on our bones, would that bring the world closer or further
apart?
Is the inception of community down to lies, for good or bad or
is it why it never started?
Even so, let me start.
Hello.
I'm blue, not your typical association to happiness or sadness
but to completion,
I crave the depth that has no visible end- like the ocean and sky
I feel so close,
I'm blue.
Who are you?

The real life we live

There now are edible sheets of gold,
Sheets of gold you can dress in,
confess in and impress in,
but these sheets of humanity guarantee not humility just
inevitability.
We consume our souls with sheets of gold, artificial pleasure,
then we question why our love can never hold together.
We eat the luxuries in our lives like gold doesn't run out, and
when it is gone, we long for the things we never gave enough
to.
We breathe like the oxygen we share is money,
spending it on things we don't need, until our lungs are in debt
and we can't make it out safely.
I guess I'm saying if you have these gold sheets in your soul,
keep them there.
They look much more beautiful within you, than in a world
filled of everything superficial and temporary.

What you owe yourself

You owe yourself diamond covered words,
silk embellished love and a heart that lives the lifestyle of a
millionaire.
You are as much of a collection of royalty and riches as you
claim,
this is your entire life,
knock the trauma down that stands as this broken apartment
and rebuild a palace of golden self- love.
Open your eyes with me, beauty is anything people decide it to
be.
You have one body, and you either love it or remind yourself
that all skeletons are roughly the same.
But you are the queen, so pick the kingdom of your life and
establish the ways in which you will reign.

Everything.

Does it make sense?
That life is a lottery we save or try to dispense.
That our mental health relies on lies, or a reality where futility
occupiers our mind with the largest size.
So, time flies, with pain that can arise.
Or the joy that eventually- dries.
We question everything like asking is healing,
like knowing is breathing.
But nothing except our souls are left dreaming.
It seems as though life is a collection of moments,
with each sentiment all consuming, like gifts or rodents,
We can't escape because our energy is the universe of our fate.
No death is not a salvation, because purgatory could be agony
with no escape, no gate,
only now is what you own,
we'll either learn a beautiful- a manageable survival or watch
this life from below while our identities drown, all alone.
As I said now is yours, do as you will,
only your perspective will save your soul from becoming-
terminally ill.

Be happy

Let go of the fire that awakens the darkness within your
thoughts.
Let go of this need for control.
You can't end this war if it's playing on the screen of your own
face, the only time you can see it is if you look in a mirror but
everyone around you can always watch this war and mirrors
aren't always available.
let go because you are not built on a system to fix the way the
world works,
or find the faults in the systems and drain your mind that you
think is operating at the expense of, finding a solution.
You're not built for the world to use.
Be happy because that's the only way the world won't use you,
but you'll use the world to understand that if you are happy,
you are free.
And then no one will be watching your eyes, because the war
has ended, and peace is not a visible advertisement.

Elastic lives

You need an elastic life,
a love where no matter how far the distance or stretch, it
cannot be cut by a knife,
a devotion that allows you to bounce back after every failure,
and a perspective that cannot reach its elastic limit because this
is your saviour.
You need to be unbreakable,
If they hate you,
adapt to accept that you do not live for their acceptance,
but do not ever cut or break that elastic for anything or anyone.
Because the truth is if your soul is not elastic anymore, oxygen
cannot slingshot you from the worst moments to the very best.

Guilty decision

Do you feel guilty?
No.
I don't mean for your mistakes.
But for all the opportunities you didn't let your life uptake,
Glowing words left unsaid.
lost late night drives into the sunrise so vibrantly red.
Ocean dives, laughter until your eyes cried.
A discovery of cities or towns recognised from your dreams.
Hesitating to risk for your passion,
To live in a timed system as a distraction,
Almost living the life, you ached for.
Because no one told you this life is yours.
Would this be your regret?
One I hope will send your soul into the life you dreamed of, and
not the life safety asked you to bet.

Losing Yourself

Breathing becomes difficult when oxygen begins to filter
through you.
 You are left with the residue of a girl who knew exactly how to
escape this collection of hurricanes before it was too late.

Your body- lost in the inversion of its purpose.
Somehow turning oxygen into an unorganised pile of molecules
waiting to be
arranged.
You finally arrange them.
You inhale.
You exhale.
You inhale another pile; you exhale another try - but this time
seconds are all you have
to rearrange again.

You're breathless.
You begin to search for your inhaler, one that can clean this
residue and bandage your cracked lungs.
One that can persuade oxygen to stay for long enough to break
free from the despair
one more time... one last time.

You begin to clench onto your bedsheets, you feel yourself slip
onto the psychologically stable floor, you hold on so tight not
even oxygen has seen you so anguished - but you hold on no

longer because deep inside you and oxygen both know you've slipped out of yourself a long while ago.

The composure of residue thickens, oxygen starts visiting less, the hurricanes themselves gave up trying to demolish you because they see you.

They see that you've done worse to yourself than any hurricane could ever do,

and you have no one to blame but yourself.

These hurricanes escort you to a start,
to start is to begin again right?

Oxygen began to filter through you, you began to clench onto your bedsheets and just like how you began to lose yourself... begin to find yourself.

Inconclusive

I don't think freedom exists nor fate,
but an epic meditator that can almost resonate,
with the spontaneous coincidences,
except they are sliced by pre-established and
universal tragedy.

Our reality

When I close my eyes and try to fall asleep there's something
that needs me to stay awake.
Something that makes my heart resemble a ticking clock
waiting for another something, to happen.
 But what's happening?
When I close my eyes to finally rest my mind, there's a
catastrophe in my thoughts,
 a warning that the seismic waves of anxiety are coming for me
and there's no way I can stop it,
after all you can't stop earthquakes from taking place,
 you just prepare to survive it, but I close them.
I close my eyes shut so tight because I seem to think that if I
could hold this world together with my intentions and bare
words maybe the darkness will help me,
 and maybe this earthquake won't split the earth of my mind in
two.
 but it always does,
and I'll fall right in the centre of obsession and anxiety and no
one can save me when even I, myself can't stop the earthquake I
started?
I get transported to the hospital of my body,
the doctors that are my hands and eyes try to heal, try to revive
my mind but I fell too deep into the obsessions and depth of
my thoughts, that my heartbeat is a tick and tock,
and tick and tock away from the final stage of this earthquake.
This something needs me to stay awake.
But tonight, somehow, I will try to sleep again.

If the earthquake comes,
 I will let it break my mind again because after all I'm still alive
and my thoughts are my prisoners now and the key is no longer
inside me
because something else has happened.
I set my anxiety free.

The more compact a space is the higher the pressure of oxygen
particles,
the more energy they have to destroy me, so I set them free.
I set us free and maybe it will be okay,
maybe this is all anxiety wanted- to be free and we just
misunderstood, and as a side
effect of keeping anxiety locked in our mind, it ruined us both.
This something needed us to survive the earthquake, to become
warriors.

Intensity and life

You can't live for tomorrow, next week, month or year, because you'll never
live.
To live is to feel now and feel it intensely.
Breathe deeply, until your lungs are satisfied, speak the words you've always dreamed
of until your mouth is dry, listen and understand until you have no questions left and
love everything until the word can no longer be defined.
And don't let love go because you fear they'll change, maybe they won't but even if
they do, right now they are everything you want- so love them now.
Don't let happiness go because you fear you'll get too attached to the feeling and that
the pain that follows will break you because, right now it's yours, embrace it like the
world is ending.
What if life isn't just a biological collection of information, but rather a spiritual composure of intensity, and we just keep dimming the light of our life?
This does mean unbearable and intense pain too, but pain is an inhibitor of time,
if we didn't have something to slow life down, how would you feel your favourite emotion, and feel it intensely?
Life's intensity is almost like your body is freezing cold,

but slowly you are warming up yet not enough for your body to return to its normal temperature, well- what if the moment before you reach that point the reactant of intensity is completely used up?

You'd feel an emptiness, right?

That is life without intensity.

Solution

If you can't escape the discomfort, pain or stress, find a way to make yourself comfortable. So that you can wait, comfortably-until it is over.

Crumbles of love

Distance only damages what isn't whole.
If you send a broken biscuit on a voyage it'll crumble at each
stop, whatever remains reaches the final destination.
But if you send that biscuit whole, whole is how it'll arrive.

Made for

If this is real, why does my mind betray its own compartments?
I cannot let my feet rest and wait because I seem to believe that
running into my mind's chaos will get me there faster, but I
don't want any more parts of my existence knotted. I trace my
fingertips on the pages of my poetry but, a world that's chaos
free will never accept me. I am sewn like a quilt of dissimilar
material and my life's purpose is to find a way for each material
to unite and remain whole.
If this is real maybe I am made for this- made to keep each
experience of a lifetime together and somehow unknotted.

Probability

I hated probability, maybe *I will love you if, unlikely to hurt if?*
If what?
This is what I hate, where there is probability there is no answer, no progression.
Maybe maths didn't teach me much about life, but it taught me this, if they show you love in probability, you will never get the answer your heart needs to be free.
Probability will give you what it wants,
 but if you allow the probability of happiness to lead your life, the only certainty you will have is the guarantee that you will lead an empty life.

Living or existing

We live but we do not exist.
Our mind immobilized in a maze we hold the key to but refuse
to use.
Replaying that song we hate until our ears no longer recognise
any different,
 and the lyrics sinking from our mouth to heart; time never
stops. Pain never ends. Wounds never heal.
Clocks show time- the time we are born, the time we live within
and the time we die. We fear those who hold weapons, we fear
criminals and murderers why? Because they have the power
and ability to grip our life and erase any mark of our existence-
but isn't that exactly what time does?
We fear the criminals who can be terminated but we are
impassive towards the killer who is nothing but untouchable. If
the demon we live with doesn't contribute with the fear we feel
as every second, moment, hour passes aren't we all soldiers?
Time may never pause but clocks will always break. Pain is
when we hope and pray that the demon of time reduces our
lifetime. Not only do we not fear, but we worship. Agony is
what I do not wish upon anyone, but subsequently isn't there
blessings? Strength, bravery and confidence will empower your
every inhalation. Pain moulds us into doctors, healers and
protectors for those inexperienced in the difficulty we endured.
Affliction may grow but whatever lives to grow dies. Wounds
are caused by actions and actions become memories. Memories
then loiter for as long as they are nourished. Quit nourishing

the memories from your wound, stop touching them and stop donating your recognition. By reminding yourself the wound dilates, but by forgetting the wound mitigates. Ultimately every wound transfigures into scars.

Wounds may never heal but scars do not bleed.

Utilize your key, keep looking the door is closer than you anticipate.

Change the melody and embrace the modified lyrics: time may never pause, but clocks will always break. Affliction may grow but whatever lives to grow dies. Wounds may never heal, but scars do not bleed.

Do not just live.

Exist and stain your name in permanent markers, on every single lyric to the melody of your life.

A connected theory

What if I told you that the orbit of the world depended on you?
The connection between each element of life classified itself as
a dot to dot drawing of
our world.
The pain you suffered when you lost the ink, surviving around
people empty of the ability to draw emotion or words into
another's soul,
it was a sacrifice losing one thing in order for you to connect to
another,
 so that this drawing would slowing take one specific form.
That each one of your tears the page, your aching heart a
template, and your sleepless nights designed for you to draw,
connect the correct dots but you had
no idea so you were scribbling onto your life plan.
That if each fingerprint could leave behind traces of who we
were, who we are and who we could be- we'd touch our world
less.
Less because we fear sharing our soul with those who could
own it, destroy it.
But we do this anyway,
every word we set free into the world spreads like a wildfire in a
forest of fear or like the caress of sunlight upon a blooming
flower.
We leave a fingerprint of our soul wherever we go,

ink stain by ink stain until we run out and our soul is completely free of our protection but even then, we can't see the trace of these stains just yet.

One day we will discover that through the lines and curves of our fingerprints together and connected we form one drawing. What if the orbit of our world depended on you?

I don't mean the orbit of this earth, but the orbit of life.

Living into death

Place upon water your heaviest convictions.
Watch.
Watch if they drown with no doubt or pause and compare this
to dropping weight into water.
 Do you think before you drown your thoughts, because if you
do within this
time you are filling up your mind with liquified turbulence and
time is the only known vehicle that can keep you afloat?
Compare.
Does a weight wait before it sinks?
Are your thoughts really a weight?
You inflate your fatal thoughts, the bigger they are the closer
they are to the end, right? But the more oxygen you inflate into
a balloon the harder it is to drown.
You don't want to drown your thoughts; you want to
reincarnate the word 'depression' into 'liberation', and you can't
set yourself free if oxygen has become your enemy.
It is as if the more you understand, the less you feel.
You can't create an afterlife while living, but you are living into
death.
Drop the weight again, this time-catch it.
You see the only reason the weight needed saving was because
it isn't designed to carry oxygen and you're the one who
dropped it, so as long as you are breathing you are filling your
lungs with life,

your brain with serenity and your soul with compassion and believe me when time refuses to keep you afloat and oxygen abandons you, you'll become the heaviest
weight at the bottom of an ocean.

Compare.

Do you choose to become a weight or remain afloat because time has one destination,
and you're heading towards its location?
Live into life because losing yourself isn't a mistake it's a choice,
 just remember the more oxygen you inflate into a balloon the harder it is to drown,
the more life you have to live.
Don't destroy what is designed to create.

To define you

His eyes are not like books, nor art or lyrics.
His eyes, a universe for which lives a million lights all differing
in brightness.
Each light a life, one to heal, help, love, challenge, strengthen,
motivate -all the purposes possible in a lifetime belong in his
eyes.
I look at them to see, what the universe has gifted me.
An entire universe in the form of two round zircon diamonds
and a gentle heartbeat.
 I vowed to be his candlelight that helped those diamond eyes
sparkle, glow and glisten for the rest of his life.
I had the universe to love and I was ready to burn completely
just to keep his flame, just to keep his soul awake.

Temporary

And all of our oxygenated realities will shatter, in between the choices of time.

Every day

What if the world was perfect?
Do you think it would really be better?
Happiness would be an everyday asset to our lives that it'll lose
its power, we would have it in an unlimited supply so would we
still appreciate it?
Love would be among the common words used and felt every
day, where would its strength go?
Pain would be an unrealistic story, and so would we dream of
feeling it if it was never there?
The world may be completely broken,
 but the beauty of that is that when the cracks are even
attempted to be put back together, the feeling is incomparable
to anything that could ever be felt in any utopia.

Healing

I used to believe that flowers were a gift but since when is
taking a life to repair a smile a gift?
I used to think aquariums were incredible but is imprisoning
sea life really that admirable?
People seem to believe that if you destroy one thing to fix
another you are a saviour, but you're only broken.
Yes broken.
It's like standing in between the crack of an earthquake with
one foot on the right and the other on the left testing which leg
will hold you, but if one falls, you'll drop either way.
It's like breaking a pill in half giving each person half a dose,
you're destroying something to help someone, helplessly.
You're destroying something either way.
That's not being a hero, it's being broken.
Be patient,
your solution will come, and it will heal you completely.

Laminar lives

Stop.
Stop asking time to stop running if you can walk.
Time doesn't understand entrapment, the desire to crawl slowly into your pain and stay there because time only knows freedom.
You can't stop a laminar cascade, and you never try, even if you can't see its movement because you know in order for a waterfall to be alive, a home, a salvation and a beauty, it needs to flow.
For us humans; to live, heal and feel requires us to walk with time into liberation- whatever it might be for each of us.

Queen and kings

Roses and thorns have never been compared to beauty and toxicity, just self-defence.

Protect yourself as elegantly as a rose, but with the power of thorns.

Nothing

Nothing stays broken forever.
The things you cannot fix are not irreparable, permanency has not captivated them.
They have just healed in a way that no longer corresponds with your attempts at renovating their damage.
A broken key?
Not even close, a brand new key unable to fit into the lock of an abandoned building.

Your medicine

I gifted you with a syringe, overflowing with the love you extracted from my veins except you injected her with every drop, perceiving that my veins were contrived for your blood.

Flameless eyes

I raise my candles to you,
not champagne glasses or wine-the colour of our passion, but
simple candles.
I raise the lilac flame in your name,
watching the flame detect the danger its own existence
possesses the ability to: mark skin for a lifetime, destroy
buildings, vanish homes, take lives, stain humanity with death
and erase years of life.
But this destroyer once started as a lilac flame used as a source
of safety,
 or the embrace of a romantic dinner,
this light source was used in occasions of celebrations yet even
when freshly brought into the world it is able to be vanquished
by one simple blow.
Happy birthday have you made your wish? Did you pray fire to
give you another year of life, or did you beg it to stop
destroying it?
The one utensil of life that correlates to us all so well.

A lilac flame

A human

Life's duet

You are in a train.
Parallel to you is a man smiling, wearing a tie the colour of your eyes.
Next to him is a man in tears, dressed in a white suit holding his daughter, and at
every laugh she expresses he sternly tells her to just be quiet.
The man parallel who is smiling seems the happiest, yet he is on his way back from a lost job, to the funeral of his wife.
The other man who is in tears, who seems like trauma has tied his heart strings is in
fact on his way to his wedding, marrying the love of his life troubled because he didn't like the suit that he chose.
And above all- you.
You are sitting parallel to the only worlds that exist thus far.
The world of the smiling man who chose to learn the happiness in the library of life's
pain and committed to heart the appreciation of all he was gifted with in this life.

Or,

the world of the distressed man who had the most priceless gift but chose to learn ignorance and ungratefulness.

Now, you, the one parallel to these worlds,

Which do you want to belong to?

Security

Unless your; weight, face, body, personality effects your health-you are flawless, do not change a single particle of you for anyone, ever.

The only rescue

Sometimes advice doesn't suffice.
Because ears are locked in ice
 and they need to pay their price.
Sometimes you can't help someone who has a survival kit built
into their own eyes,
all you can do is help them look into a mirror.

Uncommon exits

If the floor is wet, you walk slower.
 If the fire is near you run.
And if the world is ending, you hide.
You do what protects you, possibly saves you from that specific
danger that approaches.
So why are you running from the pain if it is within you?
Why are you running towards the fire if you were safer here?
Why aren't you slowing down if floor is covered in your tears?
To escape is not the cliché of running,
It is finding the matching exit to the blueprints,
the architecture of your pain.
Finding this exit may feel impossible when all doors are
indistinguishable.
Though, this exit is no door.
If your survival kit relied on doors being an attribute of the exit
plan, you'd survive on
probability.
Your exit needs not to be a door,
but the strength to create your own way out.
To dig a tunnel in your heart,
 to walk through the worst days that are yet to come,
or building a ladder for the pain to climb its way out.
Whatever it is,
create your own exit,
and don't be fooled into running from something that is within
you.

Because if it is within you,
it becomes you- unless you create that exit.

The dependence in us

I'm a rope on fire and air is my fatal enemy.
The blazing touch of my skin pushed you into the purest of
sterling waters-but I am not an angel.
I am not the configuration of any saint.
The essence of steel grey coats and layers the concealed truth
behind the unengaged theatre in my eyes, but I am not an
actor.
And as words drop from my lips, they diffuse into the polluted
oxygen encapsulated around me, but I am not a cracked
perfume bottle.
Yet I enquire, why does air despise my existence?
I can contaminate.
I can poison your ache with the blanket of comfort enveloping
my
smile-but I am not a doctor and remember that when you catch
fire and the flames become the dynamite of your world.
I did warn you.
Air is my fatal enemy.

To live or to visit

It is the design of your heart that captures inhabitants, the decoration of your face will only attract tourists.

Self- invented

If you think life's too hard, re-define your experience.
What if this breathing, feeling and finalizing capsule of time is
a dream?
Would that be beautiful?
What if this experience is a vacation until you return home, to
death itself?
Would that make it more memorable?
If you re-defined the broken words from our dictionary of
experiences, would you read its definition, or still remember
the same association, life with pain?

Abstract

You burned, just like ice freezes skin.
You cannot survive what my soul is made of,
I will destroy you with the elegance of a paradox,
beautifully poisoning,
healing your false perception of me,
by spilling lemon juice in the open cuts of your hope that
somehow, I am different.
But your understanding of different is now bleeding.
Who I am cannot be known to you,
because I am exactly what you would love to despise,
crave until your demise,
remember details you cannot describe,
until you drive yourself crazy,
because who I am cannot be confined to a single mind,
and no one but I, owns access to this shallow intensity.

Memory

We live in resolution, craving closure.
It was never about when, where or how much,
It was simply that it did.
It did end.
It did hurt.
It did ruin you.
The fact that it did concludes a part of yourself that couldn't
have continued to survive.
We become so consumed in destroying something else to
equilibrate the balance between what you lost and the anger
that you have found.
But breathe.
And,
know one thing;
Everything lives in its resolution.
If it ended, treasure that end as if it wasn't,
because that end is the beginning of how this memory will
always reignite within you.

Stains of insecurities

You have a stain on your mind that needs to change.
Clean it and erase every mark of its existence.
That stain is the eraser of your happiness, so destroy it.
But here's a secret, the only weapon able to wipe this stain is
you.
Because this is simply a war against yourself, and who knows
you better than you
know yourself?
Don't ask for compliments or reassurance on your way, in fact,
don't even look in the direction of them because *'you are
beautiful'* and *'there's nothing wrong with it'* may make you
smile, win one battle against this war, but that smile will fade
and there is a
war that requires all battles to be won.
The only way you can win is through yourself.
It may take a while but start on the first battle.
Don't compare, you are not an art exposition, which painting is
best?
There is nothing in this world that equates to your existence,
you can't compare the door of the art gallery to a world with a
heartbeat.
The second battle is understanding that those flaws and
insecurities are marks of your
uniqueness, they define the entire collection of your body's
magnificence.

The third is, you only feel insecure because what you have,
maybe no one else does,
but why are you trying to be like someone else when you are an
entire world of beauty
and potential?
There are quite a few battles awaiting you in this war, but once
you realise that you are an entire world, you'll understand that
maybe blue grass is better than green.
Maybe pink sunlight suits you and maybe when you accept that
you are rare, you'll start treating yourself like you're a limited-
edition world, and not a stain of abnormality.
Win this war,
win it for you.

The End

 Maybe you care about the way things end, or maybe you don't because well- they're
ending.
But it's the part of a story we all hate.
Finishing that series to losing someone you love; it feels like this substance is
blistering your body, at different temperatures.
The end is the silence,
the pause where there is neither progress nor change but a stagnant emotion, somehow filling you up.
 It feels as if the end is the reconfiguration of your body, your bloodstream into water.
Thoughts like plastic forks, each poking into your heart as it spills leaving your heart
beating- empty of sentiment.
But I think we should fall in love with the end,
think of it not as loss but the final puzzle piece, once that tiny detail is in place everything is complete.
Think of it as finally fixing a draw, finally it can close, gently and serve its role.
Think of the end as the reaction we show as we finish feeling everything there is to feel.
Mould the ending into fulfilment, paint it with the colour that satisfies your heart
aesthetically,
 because the end is the missing piece to our lives.

The wedding rings to a wedding, the smile to a face, the words to a book and the
purpose to a life.
We will never be able to choose how or when we will end,
 but let's choose how to feel about it.
The end isn't loss or ruination, it's the protective layer to the creation of life, so that it doesn't lose its meaning.

Faults of time

In a world where almost everything has already been said,
defined and done, happiness still hasn't found an easy route
home.
 Pain has travelled the world, settled in the countries it admired
most.
Anger has always been the transport of regret, that one missed
train or missed
airplane to the most important event of your life.
 We've spent boundless lifetimes trying to understand ourselves
but maybe,
that's what we are doing wrong.
Maybe happiness's attempt to find an easy way home was
inevitable,
maybe it is in its genes to only travel by the toughest route.
 Maybe instead of trying to keep pain in one location it needed
to travel to be able to
give us all the relief that is draped in wisdom.
 Maybe we just needed to walk through life instead of taking
the easy way out of
regret's transport.
Maybe,
we just needed to experience everything patiently allowing time
to give us life,
instead of making time limits, our life.

Savour to last

There is bitter love just like there is sweet.
There is aromatic pain just like there is flavourless.
But the best and worst thing is that you never know which
flavour of each you'll receive.
You either have to become immune to its force or indulge, for a
while at least.
Everything will eventually end, but everything that was ever
real never dies.
Some attempt to become immune to the bitterness, they can't
stand it, others indulge
until even what was once bitter to them has completely lost
flavour.
 When we are enjoying our favourite meal sweet, savoury or
sour- we don't enjoy it for long because that flavour escapes,
drowned by the liquids we choose to quench our
thirst or the immediate act of swallowing this meal, its
physically gone.
But the entire life of that meal is never just the flavour or even
the food itself- it's the
time, the effort, the emotion, the sacrifice, the memories that
have put together that meal, and when the meal is gone
everything that was sharing time-all that gave it life
will never die.
Everything eventually ends, but nothing real ever dies.
This is the reality we often forget when the sweetness of our
lives turns bitter, when we have lost complete flavour and all

seems hopeless, we always think that the end is it, but we are
still alive, just not in the ways we chose.
We want the physical thing so badly we ruin the plate, the
foundation of our lives
completely once it's gone, that plate that gives us no joy is what
has stuck by us.
When the meal has ended- the plate is still there.
When our happiness has ended, we have not lost life- pain will
keep us alive whilst joy
finds its way home.

Why can't you keep happiness?

Breezes or storms, it's still fleeting.
But weather isn't static, like your soul dynamic.
To seal happiness, compare not to the opposing, but to the
ever-growing.
And forget the way an iron erases creases, because some traces
of happiness need to be
folded and scrunched in order to survive.
Or the way clouds don't make you forget the sky, only to
heighten its splendour and perhaps the long-forgotten smile,
the one you can't miss because you cannot recall.
Just nostalgia for the memories you, can't scream for or silently
call.

Why can't you keep happiness?

Because it isn't yours to keep.
Just bandages for the wound's life cannot heal.
When you feel it, treasure it enough so that it, might want to
visit again.

Might want to stay, just a little longer.

My Home

He wrapped his arms around her like the final touch of
preparing a gift.
His arms like wrapping paper and his veins like ribbons, hands
internally packaged with the ribbons that know not only the
love of embracing his blood but displaying
himself as her treasure.
As his arms pulled away, he'd unwrap them so gently to show
the audience of their love that the gold print of wrapping paper,
is only a fraction of the beauty underneath.
Her.
These silk embellished ribbons tied around his hands formed
the image of a fence,
one to provide her with protection that within his love nothing
could ever harm her. Resting her head, the puzzle only he could
solve upon his chest, his bones, his ribs the gateway to heaven
and she listened to the wonders of heaven as she listened to his
heartbeat.
Each of his footsteps became the floorplan, the guidelines to
not only keeping her safe but keeping her inspired and she'd
follow the traces to arrive at a single destination- peace, and
here at peace the sun would set with a gold that was priceless.
When the sun set gold would become more of a world than a
style.
 A sweet elixir of heaven and reality, a formula that brings
home medicine to cure the
incurable, fix the unfixable and the breathe the unbreathable,

all with a glance into his eyes,
because he was love.
I'm the gift wrapped in the wrapping paper of his arms,
delivered at the gates of heaven with one sole purpose- to love
life unconditionally.

Human plasters

I heard the four words,
I'm here for you.
 Like each one was a plaster in a box of forty.
With ten of 'I'm',
ten of 'here',
ten of 'for' and of course ten of 'you', in illusion.
Each plaster waterproof, when you are 'here for me' no liquified
pain can get to me
and I'm guaranteed to heal without an infection of betrayal.
Each plaster made of the most flexible fabric to adjust to every
movement of disloyalty.
 Sitting on top of my open wound with free access to touch it
and stain it with your residue of lies.
Each plaster made to stick to my skin so well, that I could never
lift to look underneath and discover that, all you are 'here for
me' to do, is speak the words that in reality are the twins to
wind,
but how can I hear this wind when the plaster is stuck so tight
to my loyal skin?
Each plaster you placed upon my skin,
each of the *I'm here for you,*
you stuck into my ears had the scratches and cuts of my
wounds,
yet it was supposed to shield mine, wasn't it?
Isn't that the purpose of a plaster?
 Isn't that the purpose of a human dressed in 'I'm here for you'?

They may be there for you or they may never be,
but plasters do not heal you.
They are a fine line of protection,
and sometimes keeping a plaster on for too long will never
allow it to heal fast enough.
Sometimes our plastered reliance of someone else will never
heal you fast enough.
Remove the torn plasters and allow the healing to be done, by
just your body.
 Allow yourself to heal yourself.

Empathy and sympathy

I watched the rain drops mizzle and twirl among the others on
my pristine window
screen.
All stumbling to the same place.
A place of undeniable welfare.
The place they all passed- they all knew.
All together yet all divided.
I listened to the screaming sky as if the thunder was its grievous
alleviation of a hurt, we know nothing about.
Entreating us to soothe the affliction, but we applaud, we
disregard.
I watched and I listened beneath the serenity of silk covers and
thermal quilts, within four heated walls, in a place I called
home.
This was what it was like to live painless,
as if the world remained under the roof of an infinite cycle of
catastrophe and cataclysm, but even then in my heart I felt so
warm and as if peace was enticing my muse- a peace
manufactured at my mental expense.

A while later.

I'm watching and listening within three walls of oxygen
iniquity, shivering in the vacent cold I have to breathe.

I'm only one rain drop mizzling and twirling among others on the intoxicated window screen called earth, and this time- it's the sky's turn to watch our pains.

Limitless

I'd like to put pressure on the sun, create a dent signifying how
sometimes even the most powerful source of warmth can be
touched, but how could I ever reach the sun?
How would I ever reach happiness if I'm so far away?
I'd like to coat the moon in sand, carve the letters of joy and
watch the light wipe their
visibility away before the moon could even talk to the sun, to
show how even the most beautiful source of happiness can be
erased with a hand that intends to keep darkness suppressed.
 But how can I reach the moon if even the sun can't bare its
existence?
We fear snow because of how it affects us, but we are the
destroyers, so do you fear the thing you are in control of?
Why do you fear your own mind?
Our mind isn't as far away as the sun or dark enough for the
moon.
Do not let fear control, what you have control over.

Compass

You are your very own compass,
In control of the direction of your happiness and success,
run by the solar power of your devotion.

My lesson

I understand.
It's hard to read when no one has ever shown you how to,
It's hard to speak when you've never heard the words
pronounced.
It is hard to love when all you've felt was pain.
But do you see that there is equity here, between you and me?
In order for me to understand you, I have to have gone through
all of the above,
and I have.
I didn't know how to speak, nor read or have any idea how to
love but now I do, and I
can show you how to.
Love is a laminar effect within your heart.
The way your blood flows through your body, not at all visible
to you,
this is the mirror image of love.
And to love, recognize that although a laminar waterfall
appears frozen, it is moving. Love is there, just touch it.
Speaking is like the wind, some days there is a subtle breeze
that refreshes the heart of all who can hear, but other times
speaking becomes a storm, these words will crumble and break
everything until your mouth is empty and you notice your life is
too.
To speak is like nature, just choose what you want to do with
the life around you.

To read is like magic, you have the power to view the mind of another soul; to

empathize, to unite one heart with millions and identify that unity is what creates and

keeps us truly living, through pages, words and love.

To truly live all you need to do is open your soul and allow the greeting of another through pages, words and love.

The danger of expectations

I didn't expect to breathe in broken dust particles or breathe in beautiful damage- but expectations don't understand anything.
I couldn't really see what happiness looked like,
 I thought it was smiles and light, but when I saw a man who's clothes looked like broken dust, smiling at anyone he saw, with tears falling so pure, I knew that happiness couldn't be that, because even though he smiled, his heart seemed styled to accept that all he was going to be was- broken dust.
I couldn't really see what pain looked like either.
 I've observed people in pain, and it seemed like mental, physical loss of naturality or a gain of unfamiliarity,
but when I saw a woman battling the worst disease, I knew pain couldn't be that because she laughed with tears of joy so damaged but so beautiful.
 She reassured her husband to never let go of the magic from hope's everlasting ties.
 And here we are, the few of us who aren't homeless or sick, just empty of the life we want but don't have.
We are the ones who breathe the broken dust particles and expect damage to not be beautiful.
 Pain doesn't have to be the only way we can value life and happiness doesn't have to be the only way to enjoy life.
Expectations don't understand anything,
just like our expectation of becoming happy someday,
 doesn't understand that there is this very moment that can become- more

than that, if we let it.

Approval

Tracing your cold fingertips through her hair,
 into her ear you repeat the words of a thousand,
 let your guard down with me, let me take down these walls
you've built,
 but why?
What's a home with no walls?
What's a prison with no guards?
What's a castle with no protection?
Why do you encourage your lovers to undress their
vulnerabilities in a world where walls are needed to keep
warmth inside?
Where prison guards are needed to ensure safety.
Where castles are decorated with globes of guards on every
branch.
Encourage your lover to build a door in the wall.
Encourage your lover to introduce you to the guards.
Encourage your lover to clean an empty room of a castle and
allow you to accommodate.
Encourage your lover to protect themselves and walk soul
naked only when
the choice suits them.

In between

I know what it will feel like and I'm not ready,
 I'll never be ready.
It will feel like my body and mind has separated
My mind in a different room to my body
both rooms locked
transparent walls, glass windows
Soundproof.
It will feel like I'm screaming for my heart to be connected to
me again
but it can't hear me.
No matter how loud I scream, what words I choose, how much
I'd promise my heart to never let anything hurt it again.
I will never be able to set my heart free from that room or
welcome it home.
But the truth is even if I did get my heart back,
I wouldn't keep my promise,
I'd put my heart right back into your life again.
Loving you is heaven, losing you- hell.
 But I guess if you left the earth,
you'd leave with my heart,
 and that isn't heaven or hell,

but the empty space, in between.

Number one

You have to believe that you are the greatest.
The latest, best, most spectacular innovation, all defined by
your name.
You have to believe that you are the one,
Rarer than the rarest flower.
But you have to believe that you are more, always so much
more.
The flower, soil, the sunlight and water.
Your growth, inspiration, happiness and strength- like organs
within you.
You have to believe that you are free,
even if your heart's cables connect to someone,
or your minds pathways have been walked upon.
Especially then, when you are kept,
 believe that you are in control, and you will be.
You absolutely have to believe in your own life, you attract
what you display.
Bees to flowers, magnet to magnet- your dream to you or your
fears to reality.
You have to believe,
 because as long as you believe, the world is yours and nothing
can capture you.

Goodbye

All it took was one phrase that required two words to mean
what it does.
You took a word of euphoria and positioned it among a word
that's aching,
 and somehow, it's meaning belongs in both those categories.
So why is it that when you say good-bye two people separate
but the two words remain whole?
Perhaps the *good* in front is a subtle reminder that even though
we are losing this future, we've gained moments we can relive
in this present,
and the *bye* behind alerts you that behind you will live a million
memories in the form of your decision.
All it took was goodbye and you'd think a missing piece would
create an empty space, but this goodbye didn't leave me empty,
it left me full.
Too full of what life could be and I didn't even speak both the
words-goodbye.

We wasted time.

When we thought the world ran like a straight line.
Deception, rejection, momentary satisfaction to a heart's failure
at the attempt of love's resurrection.
None of this resembles a straight course, just a curly, circular
and disfigured force.
I hate them,
no, you don't hate anyone, you hate the intention that the one
you loved lost direction, while you waited in an empty
construction field of unrequited love.
They hurt me,
 no, they didn't hurt you, they hurt this little plant of love that
grew within you, fed from their heartbeat and now that they
hurt it, it has hurt you too,
so, let that plant die.
Yes, it is beautiful, I know, but the roots are just too toxic.
Let go and you'll be free.
Everything is hard, I know.
 Nothing worthy is easy, nothing special is an essential and
nothing fulfilling is worth fearing.
If you want it that much, fight until it's in your reach to touch.
We wasted time complaining, overthinking and resurrecting
the love we miss,
that it is as if we have forgotten that the real worth of life is-
timeless.

Life bonds

There is this undying fascination about fireworks that keeps the whole world's eyes
fixated upon glitter and colour stained skies.
This moment of fascination that will appear to dim within two seconds of its departure.
Like fireworks the beautiful things in life sparkle so bright they light up your world,
but after a while they dim and there's no more explosions because eyes and colour have become way too familiar.
Like a freshly ironed relationship,
the newness of mystery the undying intrigue,
the hope to watch those fireworks explode relentlessly into the sky, die within the
creases of familiarity.
Almost like a sweet aroma of tasting a delicacy, the fireworks of flavour explode but once your taste buds meet the flavour too often, the fuel is just ingested.
And sometimes we pay so much money to watch them explode into the darkness that we tend to forget that if the show is cancelled and the fireworks are off, perhaps we could get to know the sky's real colour.
Perhaps we could form bonds that do not dim with time.

Decisional truth

There are attributes of the world we have no knowledge of,
 perhaps the imaginable isn't real because we are aware,
for this reason, perhaps the unimaginable is the reality
because well- the world needs its secrets to keep us alive.
What if the splinters we get are a source of punishment, our
doors have had enough of the constant division from its home?
 Just as we divide our happiness from our lives
leaving it an orphan,
because we cannot find its place in our lives?
Perhaps paper cuts are a warning, for always tearing apart a tree
with anger, because
we are tearing apart our own source of life.
There are lives all around our oxygen, that we know nothing of.
And the tragedy within this truth is that some limits cannot be
exceeded.
Whether you read this on the date of which it is written or a
million years later, you are
human- you will never escape this limit.
 It is so achingly beautiful because this way we have a million
years to figure out how to be human and be human well.
We just need to start somewhere- let's start here, with your
world.

Innovative pain

Let it hurt.
Let it flood your body like a shipwreck at storm.
Let it restrict your access to breathe for just a moment,
enough for the pain to fill your soul,
 but not quite enough for it to stay, as you catch your breath.
You let go.
 This is a minor realization that pain has to teach you, to let it
in.
Welcome it, make it feel at home,
 this way it'll feel like a visitor and will leave before you could
even ask.
Don't make pain feel like an invader
an enemy because,
 I promise you now- it'll become just that.

The triumph of falling

Most people want to own some sort of power,
some form of mystery that makes them untouchable, but it's
always taken away.
The key to keeping it is falling only a quarter way down.
There are wells of pain that will force you to fall,
but no one can ever push you if you choose to jump.
And when you jump, jump close to the walls of this well.
Yes, you will have bruises, scrapes and deep cuts but nothing of
you will break.
When you fall don't close your eyes because with every quarter
way down,
you will hit a step close to the wall, step on it- grab it.
Because the power you have always dreamed of is like a step
expect in the middle of a
great depth, a well of pain.
So, own that pain, hold it, feel it become familiar with its
presence to learn exactly when it is time to step on it, and
prevent its fall to you.
That's the only way you'll become untouchable, powerful.

Chains of the heart

The world's darkest and most beautiful art is destroying one
another.
We create this little plastic mould in one another's hearts,
promise to fill it up with grains of sand until the shape is
complete and we have completely fallen in love.
But we sometimes run out of sand too soon or we feel as
though the sand would look
better on a beach of betrayal.
We spend months looking into each other's eyes transmitting
love through a
greeting of two souls,
to later buy a glass and place it between- but you have to be
grateful because you can still see each other's eyes.
You can still see each other's eyes until one of you decides to
replace it with a two way
mirror.
To watch them live without you,
while when they look towards you all they see is
themselves- they don't even see your eyes anymore.
When they become fearful of losing you, they tie your mind to
the door handle as you watch people come in and out of their
lives.
Though other times you are so caught up on the ropes they
tried to keep you tied with, that you never looked to see what
they were attached to-nothing,

but you didn't walk away, you tried to untie yourself to be free
in case they needed you- when they left you in need of help.
The world's darkest and most beautiful art is destroying one
another.
If we were made of glass not one person would live unmarked
and uncracked.
If we were made of cotton not a single person would live with
the same softness their entire life.
But we are made of bone and flesh.
We are strong enough to live marked and not as soft as cotton,
 so why don't we try to create art from a love as permanent as
the paint stained
upon the canvas?

Immeasurable distance from damage

She is the ink within a pen you can't touch or can't see unless
she decides to be known.
She is the ink at the tip of the pen, if you choose to touch her,
you'll become stained for a while, and the attempt to erase her
will only hurt your skin.
She is more than you'll ever have but less than you'll ever know.
She is the image of perfection and ruins, all gracefully twirled
into the shadow of a silhouette you can't reach, and the
sculpture of a face frozen to hide her cascade of thoughts.
Words and poetry that are the steam of her mind,
yet if you try to touch them your skin caress's a page with
imprinted words.
You can't touch her; she'll always be virtually there.
 Her mind far and her body further.
 Further away from stained fingers, corrupt mentalities,
disguised bodies and judging eyes.
That, is her power.

You can't.

Why?
Because there is no possibility.
What if that was the answer?
Would you carry on fighting?
Probably if your life's substance was at risk.
But what if you tried everything, and you just couldn't,
because you can't?
Would you adapt to that answer?
A life of everything you could do- exempting what you can't
with grace, or would you deny it, thinking ceaselessly that you
can?
But you can't.
So, it ends where it began,
why?
Because who you are is defined by the belief you started with.
Has it changed?
If not, this is you.
You can't escape anything within this life,
because you can't,

what ~~can~~ will you do?

Bracelets and kindness

Imagine your life as a bracelet- the chain type.
You have several loops at hand and it's personalised.
You have different shades of each colour, design and shape for each loop.
The only problem is that, you don't choose these, but your life does.
If you've hurt, you'll get the sharper loop.
If you've damaged, you'll get a few faulty loops,
and if you destroyed well, you'll end up with too many broken loops that your bracelet
will no longer want to be worn on your skin.
But no bracelet is irreparable,
 all you need to do is be a person as wholesome as you want that bracelet to be.

A blind salesman

Sold.
It was the auction of dreams,
starting price sacrifice,
bidding at the life you had but,
wasn't enough to suffice.
Sold,
your dream has sold.
It was the house of your experiences,
incomplete moments releasing your soul with ease.
You began to sell.
The furniture that made the interior décor of your mind,
 carpets that softened your pathway all hardwood now, an
unprotected fall.
You sold the home of your mind.
 Falling not only onto hardwood floors, but into an abandoned
house.
And while your businesses in life began to thrive,
you wanted more so you fired all the
workers within love, but you didn't sell love, it sold itself.
All because you never stopped wanting a world you never really
knew enough to want. Chasing the life advertised to you
because it wanted to consume your soul,
potential and mind, while you thought lifelong fulfilment was a
momentary consumption.
If you've already sold your world,
it's never too late to fight for what time could never really sell,

but even if some things are priceless, the world doesn't belong to you.

And nothing has labels so, keep your world, stop selling the life you need.

Trapped in freedom

Stop letting people tell you how to feel,
splinters are almost invisible,
yet it's pain that they reveal.
Don't let expectations waste your time,
if you like your fruit whole, don't slice to impress.
Understand that morality is a concept.
You are not evil or ruined just because your life isn't one others
accept.
Rules run the world because of illusive yet collective stability,
simplicity and strength financially.
But we all know this illusion is deceptive mortality.
Populations build and individuals break because power is a
soul's diseased outbreak. And people heal through love and
profits, and let anything die that doesn't fit
into their favoured reality.
Nothing is easy or whole in its entirety, because somehow
settling is losing, happiness is confusing, and healing causes
bruising.
What pathway through this world should we be using?
Well, any life that offers the following;
Time as stability,
love as unity,
kindness as a cruciality,
respect as a community,
gratitude, positivity and acknowledging that mistakes are not
finality.

Now we can live freely except,

not really.

Confirmation

I could live a million lives,
meet love in a million vitrines,
 and converse with happiness in a million languages of a million
generations,
but my soul would never alter with the feelings you signed into
my heart.
Like a pen and paper,
a confirmation of eternity- I do.
And you did, you confirmed that this love is an eternity of you
and me,
and happiness and everything, we could ever be.

Stationary travelling.

Let's travel through life from wherever you are, stationary.
We are at the airport,
the terminal of exhilaration,
to board you need a passport of dedication, the tickets of
strength and the minimum luggage weight of pain.
We land in the country of fulfilment,
to leave you must try a million things until your soul is
awakened,
the only way out is to name your passion.
So, we catch the boat of pain named joy,
 becoming lost in the ocean and the only way back to shore is
recognising that your anchors of pain stop you from moving,
healing.
And so, we explore a nearby forest,
 plants with medicinal properties,
and create the single pill in the world able to heal anything,
do you take it or save it for someone else?
 Here, you find yourself.
This is your stop, the place that you feel at home in,
electrifying your mind with inspiration,
tranquilizing your heart with peace and sprinkling euphoria
into your lenses.
 Whoever or wherever that is for you,
 don't travel to it,
this is the one thing you should travel with.

If you made it here, passing all restrictions and all rules, your soul is free.
Travel safely.

Fighting to breathe kindness

Tidying your entire heart won't make him love you if he didn't
when you your heartstrings were knotted.
 Giving her what no one else has before, won't make her stay
loyal.
Giving your enemy the ways to win through life won't stop
them destroying what losing left you with. It's hard to hear that
even when you are begging people for one word they say they
can't speak, while they speak novels for those who didn't ask for
anything. No matter how great your heart is, human cruelty
will never let you breathe without at least trying to cause you
respiratory problems.
 I wish I had a cure for the disease that kills more than an
unhealthy body, but no poetry will ever stand a chance to stop
your hate, anger and pain from breaking everything around
you.
 I just want to say a few things to ease the pain- not cure it.
If they left you I am sorry, but I promise something will find
you and fill your wounds with plastered love. If they abuse you
please hold strength and understand that those who tare pieces
of you apart are slowly throwing you away, no one tares pages
from the part of their story that they want.
Let go.
If you are lonely and no one is hurting you but your past and
yourself, nothing I'll say will reach you if you don't let it.
Open your heart to my promise: that whether you love or hate
the ocean,

118

your life is like one, so let it be calm, beautiful, let it resemble the sunset on a summer evening because the winter in your eyes can be melted by this sunlight.

Stop creating storms to destroy the ships of relief, stop giving life to the sharks that you hope will scare away everyone who wants to laugh, love and help you, and I promise you will begin to find liberation.

There are people that will want to break you, but never forget that whatever made them so cruel still lives within them like holly leaves sitting on their heart, they are hurting too.

Not everyone can hold pain, others just want to feel the relief of handing it to you to hold for just one second, but they forget that you are still holding it.

I will end this with one thing, we all find a million ways of escaping our pains but why don't we just find one way to stop destroying each other? Everything wouldn't be so bruised, and yes, it's not easy but neither is the success of your greatest dream and that's never stopped you from fighting for it. So, what makes living in a better world any different?

Intertwining

To breathe has never felt so clean,
Like ocean air into my soul- a dream,
I have never known or understood the feeling of souls
intertwining,
but you're the first touchable image, two souls manufactured
for one another.
Like every singular grain of sand that formulates the ocean of
my body,
every individual particle of oxygen that forms in the
atmosphere of my love,
or every distinctive bead of rain that constructs the necklace of
my world's time.
There you are.
 A million rounded shards of my soul's heartbeat.
 A million rounded shards and all the million immobile cells-
together we have become a lifetime.
Inseparable souls with an indissoluble love.

What I'd do for you

These bones you call my fingers, I'll re-mould into trees to give
you life.
Each leaf as delicate as the look in your eyes when you say it
hurts,
but I have palms,
keeping each tree secure and each leaf safer.
What I'd do for you is not destroy,
not harm to heal you and not to break, but to give you life.
Piece by piece,
leaf by leaf until my palms can no longer hold these old wrinkly
trees up,
 I can look at you and see- a man with an entire life as epic and
as powerful as his oxygen.

Nothing

Years pass and you realise nothing is yours.
The sphere you held, aged into a rectangular strand of parting,
sliding through the gaps in between your fingers.
But this nothing, is wonderful.
It allows you to always have space for the meaningful.
Losing the masses of cemented thoughts, solidified homes of
self- harm, all can now slide
through the gaps in between your fingers instead of- through
them.
These gaps have always been there and no it's not that you
didn't see them,
but you refused to understand that those gaps are your,
freedom.
Curl your fingers to write the pain away, clench your fingers to
express the struggle you feel every day.
Point your fingers at the destination you want to go to and stay.
 Spread your fingers and watch the way the space enlarges.
There is more than enough space for any ache to slip through,
but your goal is to not clench when your greatest happiness
slips, if it was the thing that glued your fingers together.

Holograms

If right now was a hundred years later,
or maybe it will be when you read this.
But if it was,
and the latest invention was a hologram, replicating the exact
image of human life down to faultless voicing and gestures.
And you had one chance at it.
Would you choose yours to be them?
Even if you couldn't touch or feel them?
Even if you knew they weren't real?
Even if the last time you could see their hologram, would be an
echo of their last words to you?
 If you had no doubt that your answer would solidify at yes, ask
yourself why?
 Because this hologram is no different to your mind alone.
 You never saw this person, or heard, or felt them and yet you
chose to re-live the desire of your imagination -to have them
back again.
 Why do you crave this emptiness to fill you up so badly?
This idea of the love you thought was real is a hologram of your
unhealed soul.
Of your reluctance to understand that the moment you spent
watching that hologram was a moment lost with a real person,
who could really and truly have loved you.
They were always a hologram.
Let go of this 'nothing'.
Let it go.

Let
go.

Myths and waves

I was told that love comes in waves.
One love may feel like a tidal wave, submerging you into the
idea that love is drowning.
Another may be like a capillary wave, rippling into every other
aspect of your life, your work, your mental health, but is not
powerful enough to quite make it even into a, wave of love.
Lastly there is love like wind waves, altering your life based on
how forcefully their heart and soul's wind blows.
I was told that love comes in waves that are destiny.
When I was ready to dive into the ocean and lay floating into
these waves of love, you
came to me.
A calming light, a glow soft and peaceful.
An hour where time escaped me and though my body suffered
the turbulence of these waves, I didn't feel anything except the
glow within my soul.
It turns out, love is not waves- it is more like a sunset or
sunrise.
Endless peace that decorates your soul in the colours of heaven
and for a lifetime.
That is love.

Forgive

Forgive, we all make mistakes.
As long as we breathe, we all break to be fixed.
But never forgive to the extent that forgiveness becomes acceptance.

Circular

I'm confined in a cylindrical form of a lifetime
slipping through a tunnel of thoughts
travelling in a circular motion of beliefs, scenery and sounds
a circle is my silhouette,
any sympathy?
The round wafer-thin outline that schedules my daily voyage
and the satirical curve that pushes me into accompanying it on
its continual rotation are both yours too.
A circle is our silhouette
what about now?
Except this outline is a mirage,
one we recognise by the names limit and restriction
our satirical curve is our minds protection against the ambition
piercing edges of a square
rescuing us with round cushions from the lengths of a
rectangles path,
a circle has no edges
no straight sides
no end
but this life does.
Remould your daily words and eliminate the desserts of
familiarity
unfasten your seatbelt too
strut towards your most feared lifestyle.
To a square, a triangle-any form of a lifetime that feels foreign
because the most ravishing life is one that ends,

one that pricks your mind on its edges to form a crack so minor yet large enough to be filled with new experiences beliefs, scenery and sounds.

 Permit your feet to walk straight ahead-this way you'll never slip in your tunnel of limitation.

Substitute your mirage for a hologram of reality,

if you never discover the pain of an edge- you'll never discover the difference between a mirage and a hologram.

You'll never discover why pixels can't make a perfect circle.

You'll never discover why the shape of this life is worth every breath in the escape of our handcrafted circle prisons.

You'll never discover why your life is the exact way it is today.

Our euphoria

Sugar?
No healthier, he's like honey.
 Love?
But deeper than love's definition,
he's like an entire dictionary of love's synonyms.
Amazing?
Underestimates him,
he is astounding.
My words to him walk out of my mouth with ribbons and pearls
in their design,
 each word perfectly packaged to open up into his ears,
 like every hour in love with him, a gift.
My smile to him feels like velvet and glass glitter, when he
touches my happiness his fingers brush through soft velvet, but
when anyone else tries to take it, they'd cut their fingers on
glass in the silhouette of glitter.
My eyes with him, imagine nothing, because if he is my eye's
view, heart's householder and mind's companion, there is
nothing in this world I'd wish for.
To him, I feel like life has a purpose grander than fences of pain
or gates of superficiality, but rather of a kingdom where I am
the queen of my life and he is every
particle that makes up this kingdom.

A Compass

For fifteen years I have built myself a compass for the directions
of my mind and heart, all for the fear that if I left the walls of
myself for too long, I'd, lose my way back.
I would travel all over the globe.
Through continents of happiness, countries of desire, cities of
love to towns of fulfilment.
Through the pleads of time I became a traveller of emotion, all
with my compass.
But I came home one day,
because no continent of happiness was big enough for the way
you made me feel.
Your words became the illumination of my sky in a storm,
 if I was out at sea the waves would fight for me to get back to
shore.
 Your eyes became my orientation,
I looked at them and saw what direction I needed to head
towards,
and it was always love, but greater than any cities I'd ever
travelled to.
Just like that, your existence became like an aerial view of the
city lights in an airplane window, while I was with you, I no
longer saw what direction my compass, but now I saw the
entire world in one view- you.

Catch with open palms

Today I caught a moment.
It didn't last very long in the grips of my palms, but I caught it.
For the time in which this moment was mine.
In this moment I looked at myself and saw everything I have
ever wanted from the world.
 I felt not full, not empty but the perfect balance in between.
I knew of the ending but felt nothing of the pain of losing it,
I just held on and felt everything that there was to feel.
Then in that moment I knew why being alive was such a
blessing.
But I'd only found out this secret,
 once I stopped,
and with the moment slipping through my fingers I saw it.

To be yourself

There is a vigorous distinction between actuality and idealism.
Flowers have been adored for as long as they have existed, from
the most exquisite roses to the unbeatable polyester tulips.
 I was stuck,
stuck between what was more arresting, the roses or the
polyester tulips?
 Then I comprehended; the polyester tulips are fascinating,
beautiful and will last forever, but that was the issue- they
aren't real.
The roses require effort; providing it with sunlight and water to
remain healthy and to flourish, the roses require time, patience
and commitment.
You sacrifice the most incredible gift to keep the roses alive,
time, but for the tulips, you admire the perfection and
flawlessness and that's it.
Although the tulips were my dream, perfect idea of a flower and
impeccable beyond compare, that was my beautiful fantasy, but
this is reality and in reality, we cannot survive in our
imagination.
In actuality the roses were my beautiful eternity.

Incomplete existence

Part of me feels like a book with empty pages, the other half of me feels like a full book, and no idea that it is full of empty lines.

Self-control

I'm a bowling ball.
Your customized and modified catastrophic armament.
I'm thrown across the bowling floor with fierce expectations to dismantle the stability and strength of every strand, even before I was touched.
Rolling down I was the new student in the class of destruction, but beginners emerge into the masters of their profession and so, the more I was strained, the more I was obligated the faster I enhanced my capacity to murder our favourite accessory in life. When the day of illusive accomplishment surfaced, I struck every pin and every pin
toppled to the ground in hysterical laughter.
 I struck every single pin,
 while every pin assembled our favourite accessory in life, and for me my accessory was, happiness.

Change

You claimed you could repair bones better than anyone, regardless of how damaged and sabotaged they may be. I rested the serrated segments in the palm of your hand more amiable and benign than I've ever been. Ultimately you positioned every piece in the correct place, but sometimes even the correct place can lead to demolition. It took you no longer than a nanosecond to diverge the bow and face me, but a weapon, any weapon is of no use without a killer. I held the arrow elevated and smiled with a confidence I have never touched as the words glided from my indignation stained lips: *I gave you the chance to release the arrow once before and you missed.* Not by coincidence or fate but because you weren't prepared. You weren't prepared to sacrifice your heart. You claimed you could repair bones better than anyone, but you never claimed that you could repair yourself.

Again

The word we all wait for with passion or strain,
 again,
another life we reign,
same rules with a different uniform,
a soul within a celled suit.
Ironic, because we crave informal pursuits.
The ones that liberate our soul from our body, our mind from
our universe and our
identity from expectational roots.
 Again?
Maybe no exact replica is the same.
But again,
you desire something that has passed,
you ask, again?
Not quite, nothing will be the same, ever again.

Blame

It is easy to say you blame me or it is all my fault,
but the ocean is never blamed for its quantity of salt,
just acknowledged and understood.
Skin isn't blamed for being so delicate, or our organs for being
too intricate.
And neither is nature for being so destructive and yet beautiful,
nor our world for being so overfull.
I mean you can blame but- blame keeps pain the same.
 It is easy to say I blame them but harder to say let's listen and
understand how to fix it
or adjust our view.
 That is so much harder because it requires one thing people do
not want in painful
moments- realisation.
To realise that blame is like oil on water, sitting on top making
it heavier to realise
that to find the answer it requires adjustment and modification.

Dear world,

Do we really get old?
Or is our soul too heavy for a body to hold?
Is life at an auction until you age, or has it already been sold?
Do we really know life?
Or do we only know of one genre, so we choose to experience it
on repeat?
Is vision even real?
Or is the world's imagery just the way we feel?
Is belief a vow for the certain?
Or a worship of hope, covering the pain with a worded curtain?
A hundred questions and a thousand responses.
A million wars and a billion deaths.
Dear world,
you're destroyed because respect has turned into
disagreements,
and disagreements into war and war into death.
Today and maybe a million years from now,
 life is and will always be a battle,
 just to win- another breath of power.

Distinctive

Don't compare me.
I'm essentially free of the category
that fills me like a legacy
I am not kind nor cruel
beautiful or tall
Empty of intellect or full.
I am not an element that can be defined
and if I really tried
my soul and mind
would be fined,

I am an unbroken creation.

Not one thing stained with indignation,
because I would rather be just a particle if it is whole.
Than a world if it is broken, missing its best pieces.

Tinted souls

There are some things we could never forget.
Like you and I bound by eyes like the sunset.
Sitting in soft golden glitter, sprinkled into my hair.
I sparkled for the first time.
You are so rare.
Oh, and the ocean of you!
A sweet bubble-gum blue,
So gentle to me- like my dream whirlpool of love and
marshmallow shampoo.
But the sky of your mind, cotton candy.
No.
The colour of infinity.
Where you belong with me.
I thought what a sweet world it is, a real-life paradise.

But I came here before, without you.
And the beach was just a beach.

And the sky was just blue.

Yes, my world is extraordinary, but only with you.

What is beautiful?

Beautiful is not extravagance.
It is tiny fragments of normality put together and built into what is whole.
It is a million tiny inaudible notes together forming a melody.
Beautiful is not a perfect or an unscarred image, it is a porcelain vase knocked over from children creating memories with laughter, all pieces scattered across the carpet and put back together using only tape and glue, the pieces- few by few.
It's the final vase- the cracked marks that can be seen, it's different and all the pieces aren't even in the correct place- that's beautiful.
Beautiful is not extravagance it is strength.
An image of fighting the struggles and standing as if you've never been knocked over.
That is beautiful.

A mistaken world

There is no formula for the way we form this era.
There are no rules for the way we rule the kingdom of our soul.
There is no insurance that if we lose a moment, we'll ever get a
replacement. Why does this heavenly freedom make us think
it's okay to destroy a part of heaven that's ours?
We cannot know what parts of the world are heavenly or from
hell,
because disguises and deception are the same thing.
If you let the world run past you on a conveyer belt,
the only luggage remaining would be pain and damaged
baggage.
Heaven was the broken bags that were left behind.
Disguises and deception are the same thing.
Don't leave anything worthy behind.

Paper cut

Slicing your morals never caused you agony,
tearing apart your soul felt like a strategy,
one to replace the psychology of who you are,
but your pain tolerance is undiscovered, so you search and-
search far. Shattering your beliefs comes at a discomfort,
a reluctance, repelling, a resistance you feel against, you are
wrong,
and you think what is so wrong about understanding the lyrics
to my own song? The people that are stepping on your
happiness because between you and them there is a difference,
they never caused your soul any hinderance.
But one paper cut, a few millimetres of slight tearing,
this reawakened the power in your morals, beliefs and lifestyle.
A paper cut.
A paper cut sometimes is more powerful than the distortion of
life.

He did

He watched.
Blind at heart but the vision of his mind, as clear as glass.
Watching is easy when your eyes aren't tethered to the tendons
of an altering heart.
 It is like breathing with perfect lungs.
But he watched, not because he wanted to own her, but
because he wanted to keep her heart unaltered,
and I'm not trying to be the one who spoils the end but- he did.

He really did.

Permanent

People are permanent stains of personality.
They won't change their mind's structure for anyone or
anything that isn't a piece that fits their mind.
If they love you, they will show you, but no amount of worry or
begging will ever change that person's structure, if they want
you, they will show you.
If they don't want you,
 no amount of sacrifice and worry or begging will ever make
them love you because people are permanent stains of
personality.
What a person wants; and what fits their morals, their
experience or their opinions is what they will do, regardless of
what paradise of love you offer to take them to.
You could give them a palace, but they'll choose the hostel that
another offered because they want someone else.
And no one's personality or mind's structure is a reflection of
who you are, it's completely the structure of who they are and
who they love.
So, don't wait, don't beg, don't worry, because if they are willing
to let you go, walk away they are gifting you with the freedom
to find happiness, walk away before they
trap you in the palace you offered them.

Hope

The role she played in this story was of equal importance to a
crystal of sugar
sweetening an entire glass of tea, but she still stirred the cup in
hope that she'd
experience the flavour of, sweetness.

Rethink and reshape

For a very long time, time was defined to me like sand in-between my fingers, unable to keep it for however long I desired.

Even happiness was defined as a temporary element, everything good has to come to an end, like happiness was a season of nature- yet one I would never see again.

And of course, love was defined as a maze-like journey, with the only way out being pain or letting go, like a fire if I wanted to survive, I had to let everything behind me burn and run.

And I did, I never tried to capture the sand grains, I just accepted that they'll fall.

Or ever dreamed of happiness when sadness had to call.

Yet I ran so far, I couldn't even see the red from the flames.

I lived with my definitions and never wiped away these stains.

But then- I met you.

And definitions were shattered, and freedom of my mind was what mattered.

You showed me that time was not unholdable, because with you, life was timeless. Happiness was not temporary but evolutionary, your soul's presence in my life turned happiness into an everyday feeling, so ordinary.

And love is not a maze, but a straight pathway, sacrifice, commitment and dedication and the ending is not pain, but a lifetime of peace and adventure to sustain. Perception is really the only definer, but you showed me that life was so much higher.

A dream comes true

When I'm with him all of life's pain fades,
and within his eyes I see the answer to love's maze,
he is the timeless love that stays,
within my soul heaven is what he out ways,
before him, yes there is always that comparison to before him,
but before him heaven was a fairy-tale and unobtainable
feeling, and now this feeling is healing my soul, never leaving.
He is the feeling of- truly breathing.

Mental health and it's twins

Being sad, is a privilege.
Sadness is like indulging in your favourite dessert, you are filling yourself up as you
eat. After it's finished your hands are empty and you just want more, except you stop.
You are full. It is a privilege to be able to stop when you feel full. Being depressed does not give you the freedom to stop, you carry on indulging in this pain even when your stomach is so full you feel like throwing up, even then, especially then depression keeps eating the emptiness in your palms.
Being nervous is natural.
It's like fearing a glass falling from the very edge of a table, it is natural to feel nervous because it is so close to the edge.
Having anxiety is not a natural experience.
It is like fearing that glass shattering whilst it's placed in the middle of the table.
Being careful is a great personality trait.
This is checking that the door is locked on your way out, making sure you drive safe, handling dangerous processes with caution or are gentle when in need of care.
OCD is not a personality trait.
It is checking if that door is locked over and over because if there's a slight chance you didn't check it properly the first five times, your family will get hurt and it would have been all your fault.

Mental health disorders and natural emotions are like twins, except even identical
twins have different experiences, personalities and perspectives of life.
And a mother would never confuse her children, so why do you- the creator of your life mistake appearances for the reality of your mental health?

Hidden blessings

If you are someone who wishes to heal all that is damaged,
here are three things you may need to know;

Damage is beauty, for the art of talent and passion.
Damage is as critical as breathing-but for growth.
Healing people is temporary, assisting them to heal themselves,
is everlasting.

Find a menu

It is poison loving someone who does not love you.
It is like drinking venom to deny the truth.
It is suicide.
Believing something you want so badly- but isn't real.
And the very worst part, is that you know it is suicide, but
accept it because you think as long as your heart dies with that
belief- it was all worth it.
Please understand- it isn't.
You have been fed crumbs, scraps and leftovers, some expired
of life itself.
You have been fed this all of your life, so you know, no
different.
But hold my hand, let me walk you into a restaurant where a
menu will be held in between your palms,
 hundreds of ingredients and so many dishes;
 flavoured joy, nutritious love and delicious treats of
excitement- all good for you.
You think poisoning your life is the only option,
because you have not tasted the cuisine of a healthy soul,
reality.
Happiness but in reality.
So, let's dine, together.

Paper Generations

It was paper love that survived.
The indented, scribbled redraft of love, the tangible sheet.
Ink stains and pencil erasers,
where pencil marks could still be seen, like air on love.
That love, paper love could never end.
It's when reality intercepts this fantasy that time becomes
shredded paper. Games, telecommunications and technology,
wrapped around our wrist like freedom to dive into our blood,
but become prisoners to our veins.
It was only paper dreams that could survive.
The novels, the art, the unbroken tears of hand-crafted joy.
Like eyes on infinity, an endless game where you and I
resonated a toy, but we are all toys, dolls or figures with roles
manufactured in the factories of our lifetimes.
Our upbringing, scripts that you either tear apart or follow.
Our experiences, new movies we either watch or skip.
Our interpretations, dreams and longings we either print off as
paper, permanency or as a video, a visual device that can break
or become famous,
until the next one is released.
It was paper love.
It was paper success.
It was paper lifetimes, that survived.

Equity over equality

Flowers of the same species each look identical, but some were grown differently.
They require a different type of care.

Sometimes heartache, is our mistake

No one in this world deserves your entire soul at the cost of leaving you empty.
Not your closest friend, your lover.
No one.
Because your soul is a mirror, it's designed to stay as clean as silver.
To reflect the light of those who want to give you toxic love before it could warm you up, too much.
Before it could make your soul too dependent on the heat that it forgets how to live through the cold when they leave you.
Your soul should only ever be touched by you, because once it's stained with other people's fingerprints you need to completely cleanse yourself, to get rid of it all.
Your soul is a mirror.
It shows those who look into it what reality is but once it's stained who you are becomes blurred and to cleanse your soul from pain is the hardest thing in the world. No one deserves your soul, but most importantly, no one who loves you will ever ask for it, they'll keep pillows underneath your soul in the case that the mirror falls.
They will help you keep it fingerprint-less.

The art exposition of all we are

His mind an encyclopaedia, knowledge that allows him to
answer all her questions. "Why do we breathe?"
He replies -"to live".
"Why do we have life?"
"We don't it's not ours, we are just borrowing it for a while so
we must take care of it because pieces of it will remain in our
soul living or dead, we just don't know which pieces we get to
keep."
Her mind is an art gallery, inspiration that allows him to give
life to his knowledge. But what knowledge does he have about
the times in which she will ask no questions, and will look at
him giving him one answer and it'll sound like; "You know how
to piece a puzzle together because there is one way for each
piece to fit, but life is a mosaic each piece is the same tile shape
except the drawing on it is different?"
He asks her, "How will I solve it?'
She looks at him, smiles and says, "not through questions and
answers, through what makes you feel both like entering a
home and beginning to skydive- all in one moment"
He understands her but doesn't understand how it's supposed
to feel.
She opens an exhibition of all the art and poetry in her soul,
letting him see how each piece is a fragment of the mosaic of
her life, her world.
Does he understand?
His eyes watering as he looks at her hands, "let's solve it
together".

A confession

The moment his ears clenched onto her words with intolerable exasperation, each loose chamber of his heart collapsed like a ceramic vase greeting cement. His stomach grasped the most terminal illness. One lung became allergic to oxygen and the other refused to take in the oxygen that kept words hostage. Is the truth always so heavenly pure? Or is it the masked poison behind the beautifully naked words?

A camera

Everything changed,
rather, everything began.
One refurbished camera.
The brightness of my eyes, I didn't know they could dim,
intensify
or even focus like a spotlight onto one thing- and blur the rest
of the world. You became the centre of my life.
The capital city of my happiness.
The orientation point if life ever spun my soul out of control.
I didn't know that my life was like some sort of photo editor,
but is isn't it's just the power of your love.
I can now crop the photos of my past, resize the camera film to
fit a million more memories of our love story,
I can edit the worst parts of my life to show me a warning or
lesson.
After all these photos are captured and my heart has edited.
You will never know that my eyes are lenses in the image of
you.
And my love the button, an automatic system that captures
every moment of your life. I am the camera for your lifetime.
One look at you,
press shoot, the camera flashes, and I see a million emotions, a
million moments.
My smile, your photograph.
I'm like a brand-new camera because my self-love has taught
me life.

Butterfly

I crave the traces of a butterfly.
Invisible touches that feel like the glistening of warm sunlight,
in the sky.
A vibrant remembrance of joy.
Lasting a few minutes like the childhood love for a toy,
an everlasting memory of a nirvana, one you can't remember
knowing the setting of, but can identify the exact creation that
came from one.
The fairy-tale of life, a princess and prince, but with age, their
kingdom fly's away and reality is what is left.
I crave for my poetry to be like one- a butterfly.
To live in your perceptions for a short while and brighten the
reality but take the
illusions and pain on- my flight home.
To give colour and design to life but also never stay for too
long, my fear of getting
caught between palms.
 I want it to be free, like a butterfly.

Unfaultable

Time teaches us the value of things.
Love shows us that life can be so beautiful.
Pain allows us to be empathetic.
Anger shows us that we are powerful.
Laughter teaches us that we are never alone.
 Passion gives us purpose.
Belief gives us hope.
Life gives us everything,
we just misuse and misinterpret.

Being alone well

Your heart will always be alone.
Whether you surround yours with the kindest hearts or the toughest,
yours will always live alone.
Our hearts are like rain drops.
Falling drop by drop.
If raindrops fell united, they'd become the epitome of a fraction of an ocean, and our heart's power doesn't fluctuate.
If each raindrop fell united it'll have completely lost its purpose.
There may be companions on some days that will offer you comfort,
like a raindrop joining another to make it bigger in size.
But after all, when it hits the floor, the harsh reality of life,
the raindrops will always
split.
Your heart will always be alone.
But it's wonderful, we can live with an entire identity that can become a world.
And if each one of us can learn how to own, protect and value that world,
we'd fall too in love with our own hearts to ever put it amongst a puddle of insecure
raindrops ever again.
This is why having an individual heart tied to no other is-
extraordinary.

The end to compulsion

Your eyes linger within the emeralds that stand as ornaments
to an engagement ring- you are yet to answer.
Yet to position on a finger,
 the vein connected to you and forever say I do.
I do see you in the emeralds that I am yet to hold and cherish
until death do us part.
Death do us part?
 Except the diamond I am yet to wear is zircon,
 emerald is an ancient artefact of heartbreak.
Your spoken mind and perspectives still feel like freshly ironed
words to my ears,
of which I wear undisciplined and the creases I try to create
fade into attempted purple partiality.
Your anesthetized touch lingers in the lost property collection
of my mind, awaiting to be found by the only owner who truly
worshiped even the piercing frost surplus of your unfelt touch,
no wonder I hated the cold.
I am sorry,
in the name of those precious stone eyes that didn't make it to
their mien,
you abandoned the only infinite lost property collection.
The only one to infinitely reserve an expanse for you,
forging it into a home in your name.
Infinitely in a world where temporarily is woven into every
written,
spoken or even drawn document.

Your anesthetized touch will someday be found in the purple string lights that hung from your walls, infinitely above me, above the foundation of us, not the ground.

The only difference is I no longer run on the electricity source of your home and this lost property collection of my mind is no longer lost nor cold.

It's found, but not by you.

It's found by the estate agent of healing and decorated with a marble interior of peace

and happiness, radiated in love.

Ladies and gentlemen, more precisely you.

 Welcome to the end of an artificial infinity.

 The compulsion has now ended.

Angel

Sometimes, I look above the clouds and wonder if your spirit
lay beneath the untouchable
Or if the colour of your eyes blended too well with the sky that
you refused to leave. That your absence would be filled with the
raindrops that fall as blue as the above from your two celestial
globes, dancing so heavenly pure across my skin,
all for my longing.
To see you anywhere and everywhere.
Forever is with me.

Heavy hearts

You're drowning.
Sinking to the bottom of the ocean.
With her tonnage too heavy to try, while she's overhead.
Above you.
Travelling the ocean on a ferry powered by your tears.
Let your fingers loosen and maybe you'll feel how weightlessly
you'll float to the
surface, how beautifully you'll glide through the sky.

My gift

She was the girl everyone referred to as ice. Not because she was cold hearted or cold minded but because she was phenomenal. The ones who claimed to love her stationed her in a room with relentless and demonic heat. Every heart who promised to heal her was too ignorant to observe that drops of her became lost along the way. The soul who promised to protect her played with her existence, placing her from chambers of the fatal cold to lethal sectors. Suffering was all her psyche received yet like ice she knew one more thing-her salvation lived in the particles that made her reversible, that the depth within her made her so unbreakable.

My Mind

Look at a coil.
A twisted path of metallic perplexity.
Physically complex yet visually simplistic.
Now enter the coil and I'll watch.
I'll see you, I'll see you twisting and falling through every curl,
but as you get up and carry on and you become so lost because
every time you see a turn you think you'll escape but it's only
another curl, another turn into the chamber of an endless
depth. Be patient with me.
From inside you will see walls, turns and corners and your hope
deteriorating as you feel like life's divorced your body and
craves freedom.
You'll see what your surrounded by and I don't just mean
physically.
From the outside I'll see just a person slipping through a coil
like a few molecules of oxygen trying to rise to the top.
I'll see a simple coil, a few turns to the exit and they'll survive.
When you come out drenched in melted hope you'll stand in
the same place as I did. *"it looks so simple from the outside
right?"*
 you will look at me and whisper,
"how are you alive?"

Warmth meets ice

Frozen icicles exchanged places with my lashes in a queue of iced bitterness and my eyes obtained a solid shield from any visible sediment.
The glittering glaciers that surrounded me formed a fence capable of withstanding any turbulence of soreness and internal vandalization.
Frozen defence was all I knew, the only protection I was familiar with.
The ice-cold air was always in disagreement with my lungs and the melted glacier water envied my vein's temperature so much that it painted my hands blue to hide them, in order for warmth to confuse me for cold and abandon me.
But I cannot survive with you winter.
Your bloodstream isn't even liquified, you tried to teach me how to breathe ice but
you became disappointed when I drowned in the weaker form- liquid.
You feed me your favourite dishes, frost- but my lips will denature it and as a punishment you force me to sleep in the source of my own nourishment, then refrigerate me into the food I consume.
I cannot survive with you winter. This queue of iced bitterness has reached its checkout and here I've found warmth.
Warmth scooped my hands into its own and I felt my heart beat again.

It was just like fire but the flame so gentle, it couldn't hurt me. Warmth's arms removed the blocks of ice from my veins and allowed the blood to stream from my river. Red fell in love with blue and blue allowed red to take its place.

Warmth's fingers interlaced mine, I could breathe again, but it was really so simple.

Heat melts ice.

So, I did.

I melted the ice shields around me, the glaciers and sediments, warmth and I became heat together and turned ice into liquid and cold liquid into warm then into vapour.

Heat will always melt what is cold. Kindness will always defeat hate.

Mind games of fear

I adore you, more specifically I adore to live inside your pacing heart, irregulate your heartbeat, send blood faster to your brain. You think I do this to stop you but on the contrary I-fear am trying to encourage you my dear, to do the thing you think I am here to stop. I send blood faster because I want to speed up the process of acting, committing. I irregulate your heartbeat to allow you to understand that you are not regular, so show the world. I am alive within you to serve you, to remind you that if you face me-fear you are one step closer to changing your world and it's all in the

name of your biggest successor. Fear.

Misconceptions of love

His cotton smile,
his touch with needle palms, full of the ecstasy of repair.
But all who craved both, felt the joy of his smile and left at the
prick of his touch. What he needed was someone who knew
that to sew a beautiful love together it requires both a pricking
needle and a cotton soft thread.

A women's soul

You thought she'd forgive you once again,
that the eyes that didn't in colour match the sky but matched
the clouds on a rainy day were too melancholic to let you go.
You were terribly wrong. You fell in love with an angel not a
lost girl. You fell in love with wings that kept her higher than
you at all costs because she can fly high enough to elevate
anyone's spirit, just like she did for you. But you always made
sure her wing became stuck to the Velcro of your pain. You fell
in love with a mind that should be scattered across the
Cassiopeia-the constellation in the northern sky. But the setting
has changed, you are now in love with an angel on earth not
heaven, and I've never known of a devil to walk through
heaven. So, to see how an angel combats the devil,
re-read the story of your love.

What is yours, is everlasting.

I am in no competition with anyone's happiness,
 because the happiness outside of my own handmade creation
is not mine,
even worse- it is temporary for me.
I will not fight for that happiness,
 it is simply the perspective that will allow you to have your
selective joy.
 I don't mean for your life to consist of heavy emotion,
impossible fates, sugar sweet indulgences in artificiality,
but the opposite.
If you are going to run for happiness,
let the destination be handcrafted,
 natural and beautiful because everything that's made within
your palms is forever tethered to you.
 The finish line to your life doesn't even exist until you enter the
starting point to self-designed happiness.

Should have done.

Your tears should have been blades to his heart,
but you settled for your tears becoming a disruption to it.
Your pain should have been a catastrophe to his world,
and you cried alone when your pain to him was like a water
droplet on the sink of his shallow heart.
Your needs,
your respect should have been as important to him as his own
eyes,
but instead,
instead your needs fell close to the pile of socks by his
nightstand that you keep washing and washing,
hoping he'll realise that they are clean again,
but he never will.
Your happiness,
should be the flames in his soul, the enlightenment to his day,
but was always simply *not now, I'm busy.*
There is no excuse when it comes to love,
no matter how deep the history,
the time together or the memories,
if he loves you,
what he should have done- is what he would have done.

Forbidden hurt

If I could imagine the forbidden aches of my heart, this would
be it.
It would feel like every ocean on this planet was drained of its
water and all the sea life
suffocated.
It would feel like the night sky to have lost its darkness.
It would feel like every shape of all objects and nature would
deform into a pile of
splinters.
Losing myself would be like a million medications out of stock
to those with limited time, like a million hurricanes scattered
across my heart,
like a war between oxygen and my lungs that never ever, ever
ended.
 Because losing who we are would be the ruination of an entire
world.
Our world.

Undefinable

It is the first time in life that my eyes and heart have become
soulmates.
When I look at you my eyes see what cannot be defined yet my
heart knows exactly
What is in its view.
A view where my mind can travel the world of literature and yet
not a single poetic
souvenir will suffice.
It is as if, with you the world has become powerless because you
cannot be compared
to a world that is defined,
and in this world only the most powerful attributes can define
you,
but your eyes and heart have no ability to speak.
To see your eyes and feel your heart is when words fall out of all
dictionaries,
and only we understand the blank pages.

Dancing in your light

To begin with,
 it didn't hurt you,
you thought of sadness as a hot cup you weren't ready to touch,
then,
a slight spillage follows- burning your heart.
Suddenly without caution you knock it over,
boiling water burns almost every part of your soul.
You scream; or cry, or shout or stress, hit, or blame, or break
everything.
You forget.
The cup would have never fallen,
 never hurt you,
if you just understood that sadness wasn't here to destroy you.
It needed you,
 because you live a life of emotions dancing among freedom.
Sadness gravitated to your light not to take it,
but dim its glow for one second- before it brightened it forever,
If you don't understand that,
sadness will stay,
and you have no more time for it,
because the dance is almost over.

Soulmate

He chose a pile of notebooks and wrote 'I am by your side' in
one,
 put it on a shelf among the rest of them.
 All these notebooks were identical all marble print with a rose
gold elegance.
 He damaged each book in the most subtle way and left the one
written in, unmarked. He watched her walk into the bookstore
and look upon that shelf,
she looked and picked up her final choice opened it and read
aloud; I am by your side. He knew her like no one else,
 he knew she'd analyse every book until she found the one with
no damage,
no sharp cuts no torn pages or a broken spine, the one worthy
of her
and he just was.

Caution of choice

I don't think you understand how powerful you are.
 How dangerous you can become to yourself.
You carry intangible weapons but all of which still manage to
touch everything within
you.
Like the guns of overthinking,
the fire of anger,
the knives of lies.
But the weapons you hold close to your soul to protect yourself
become what destroys
you, you simply kept them too close.
When the room you live in sets on fire,
 the guns are pointed to your head and the knives are ready to
come closer you make terrible mistakes.
Specifically, one of two.
You think you can defend yourself from all of them, so you
don't choose one you face them all.
Or,
 You choose to fight the one in which you believe will cause the
most damage,
You choose fire because you think you'll win against the anger
inside you and the rest you think you can outrun.
 With those choices you'll never win against the war inside you,
because those choices don't allow you to be a fighter in this
war.

The guns loaded with overthinking will strain your mind acting upon it as if your mind is elastic,
and the bullets will bounce back and forth but instead the bullets make themselves at home and your overthinking becomes the home you live in.
The knives will dig into your mind opening it up like a surgery ready to remove a tumour but instead it just opens up every fear,
vulnerability and secret to the entire world when you next speak.
Fire will choose to burn your skin.
Anger will just destroy your own skin, of destruction.
But you chose fire because it does the greatest surface damage, but the surface of your mind is like the box and inside is the jewels of your life's ultimate moments.
In other words, you chose to destroy the only weapon that could gift someone you
trust with your life.
Here's something for the next war.
Don't destroy yourself trying to protect yourself from pain,
 pain is untouchable,
 but the way in which you handle the aftertaste is a ghost you own,
 you control.
And in this war, I hope you can participate as a fighter, no a warrior.

Just a thought, if a mind was taught

I don't think it matters how many times you cut your heart
open for someone
and I definitely don't think it matters how many times your re-
open wounds if they watched a clean heart tear open and never
hesitated to stop it.
The more you question something the less you will feel it's
original worth.
And no questioning but I don't see a life of humanity on earth.
Not anymore.
Love has turned into an hourglass, now you should have the
figure of an hourglass to
feel a love that could last.
For a minute in an hourglass.
And if it does, beyond skin and physicality, you no longer live
reality.
But kindness, a sin of the ego, a fault to a man, somehow a
heart's assault.
Kindness?
No, it's just war, violence, pain and a decorated, damaged world
in the press.
It's hard to be human.
But why is it hard to be human?
If you feel something, feel it.
Don't numb the life out of your body.
If you need help, ask.
Don't let fear of judgment take your life and walk it to the past.

If you care, if you love and if you connect to another heart.
Let them know now, before death or your mistakes pushes
them further apart.
And if you discover your purpose let your soul consume your
gift,
Share it with the world because you are too great of a story to
be left untold.
Change the font and make every part of your life bold,
You only live once,
no, live a million times each as if you could only do it all once.
There is not much more to say, there's no rules to a world you
could ever know.
So just let your pain, those heavy anchors of yours go.
Stand up and begin life without them.

The respect of a soul

If they don't worship the life within your eyes, they don't deserve to live within them.

An unspoken discovery

It hurts to be alive.
You are destined to discover that happiness is the most
dangerous weapon and pain is the safest.
 This is what hurts most because you dress your face in joy,
blend your thoughts together to form the resemblance of
happiness,
 only to have it shoot once opening a wound and your bleeding
pain.
Then you heal,
 you become familiar with pain, so it gives you growth,
it kisses your forehead with wisdom and then you'll gather the
strength to enter happiness again-but you won't.
 You'll fear its suicide far too deeply,
 so, you just stay alive - and that's what hurts.

Heaven

With you the ground beneath us is made of clouds,
 I am standing on what feels like eternal peace.
I don't worry about tripping because I can't possibly hurt myself
floating in love with
you.
With you words lose power,
because looking into your eyes brings together every ache,
regret, pain, struggle in my body and melts it as if I've never
known pain,
how can words suffice?
With our fingers interlaced it feels like I'm holding the worlds
strength,
nothing could touch my heart even if it was placed outside of
my body.
Maybe everyone experiences love the same just not at the same
time,
 or maybe there's levels of love and you are given one level to
keep,
for the rest of your life.
But whatever life will give me onwards,
 so far, it's given me a love with a level that would break any
measurer,
any recorder or any doubt any soul could experience- because I
have felt a love that's resurrected every death of all that fulfilled
me with happiness and hope,
but not only that.

This love has taught even the new-born parts of my soul how-to walk-through life with clouds under my feet, even when I am alone.

 With your love in my soul,
 heaven is the oxygen I breathe.

Medicated minds

To be hopeful.
 A capsule of a placebo advertised to you as healing a soul's
wounds -taken every day with a schedule that's never
interrupted.
Each day you place the pills on a different shelf.
Yesterday it was on the window seal,
you looked at the window and saw a broken handle,
but you were cold, and you couldn't shut it,
you didn't call for help.
You used your hands,
a few tools and a few assumptions and you were able to keep it
closed for the night.
Today you placed the pill on a desk for it fell into your draw of
photos you've long forgotten.
 You looked through them remembering the love of those who
always drowned you in the dissolved pill of your hope,
 to the pictures of those who now lay their mind in pills that
resemble freedom,
and so, you began to travel again,
this time not somewhere else but to your true self.
Tomorrow you will place the pill on absolutely anything and
you'll still not take it. Because that pill was never hope,
it was the initiation of who you are.
Because you are hopeful.
You never lose belief even if you stand 0.1% chance of survival-
you'll fight.

Even if your hand could heal at a success rate of 0.01% you'll give your entire arm's strength.
Even if they said the world is too broken to be fixed,
 you'll stand on this world's ground and say - you can't break anything with a heartbeat you just alter the pattern of it- and that's why I'm hopeful,
because we are hope.
 We are just scared of pain to believe in salvation.

Voicing their silence

You love her with fear- which for you means your reflexes come
before her.
She reminds you of fire, so you never keep your hands on her
for too long- but that
doesn't stop you trying to put out this fire.
 If she speaks of ice your mind numbs at the frost you think her
words unveil.
If she shows you self-control you flinch in case she keeps you
somewhere you don't
want to be- in love.
With your fear of love your impulses destroy her.
Think before you move.
Think because she warmed up her heart to your temperature
and you froze it -you
broke her.
Think because when she stands in fire your reflexes won't help
her,
and she'll burn into the ash of your regret.
You had no idea, you were clueless.

Illusions of the heart

He contemplated me as if I was an unopened box.
Admiring the artificial illusion of the box containing everything
his heart and mind craved.
His illusion was so indestructible that it took control over his
life;
he sat by this box for months, protecting it, keeping it safe and
unharmed.
When the day came to open it,
he,
recklessly teared the exterior layers negligent as to what
destruction was caused to
the internal box.
The beauty of the flames in his eyes evanesced into the
waterfalls of reality.
His findings were ravishing, prepossessing and simply beautiful
but his eyes
however, begged mystery and the box, what it held was no
longer his souls desire.
He threw the box and the remains were left to decease into the
callous heartbreak.
He never loved the box; he loved the delusions that blinded
him.

Unwritten

I have two eyes and yes, so do you.
But through mine I see life differently well, not too different.
 Through my eyes life isn't a game but like one there are three rules;
 the characters are either,
living,
breathing,
or in-between, dying.

There is no way possible to break these rules,
That's what makes it unlike any game.
There is no escape.
But being trapped behind the barrier of its definition can be the most beautiful adventure.
One that makes the being trapped part so painfully great.

For him

For you and with you I see the pavements as so tough to protect
us from falling under our vulnerabilities,
 with you I don't see them as simple ground to be walked upon.
For you and with you I don't see laughter as an exclamation of
joy but rather as the melody with a thousand notes of love.
For you and with you I don't see the rain as cold and dreadful
but rather as a revelation of truth,
so that when we and all lovers stand in front of one another we
fall in love with our real selves clean of all secrecy and
suppressions.
For you and with you in this world I feel powerful like the
pavements under me.
I feel the melody of your laughter give me life.
 I feel that the real me is more than enough for a world that's
beauty is created from more than you and I can give.
Together in laughter and with truth we'll forever hold strength.

Renew

Every month, week or year we start a new life.
A life that's made brand new because it's been refurbished or
maybe the content is the
same but the packaging is now different.
Like a supermarket soup,
 a brand you always purchase every week,
month or year, there is less sugar or maybe there are no more
added preservatives.
Whatever happens to that soup
 it always starts a new life because it changes
and so do you,
whether for us we start a life tomorrow without a loved one,
or start a life in a completely different job,
 location or emotional state we are starting a new life.
 A life that has something more, really, we are never in
complete loss.

Our holographic love

I can't help but notice that the sparkle of a holographic
rainbow is of the same excellence
as your radiance.
Your mind shines like the silver undertones, yet your rainbow is
only visible to those
who can adjust at certain angles of your persona.
I can't help but notice that when I look at you, I feel like the
definition of happiness
cannot match the depth of love within my heart,
it is as if my entire soul has become gloss covering your heart,
letting you shine and keeping you protected from any
scratches.
A combination of;
peace, joy, love, adventure, safety and euphoria in the display of
curled colours, intertwining to form one holographic image,
you.
The most miraculous and astounding image.
My soulmate.

A little strength, boundless.

There is pain that silences you,
your mouth torn from your face and your body thrown into a
tunnel.
It is disguised as denial- shapeshifting into every other emotion
until it consumes you,
like wax and fire.
There are moments you wish this could be just pain because
then at least you knew it
by its name.
There are days when this pain will give you a million reasons to
scream but you stay
quiet because you need to know that there is greater pain than
this to scream to. There are weeks when you'd rather spin your
life through a tunnel hoping to make it dizzy enough that it
forgets the pain it digs into your soul,
 leaving you empty.
But there never will be,
there will never be a cure to the thing that silences you,
if there was, you'd be able to speak, shout and scream.
And if you could,
this would be the greatest pain, losing hope in healing.

Commitment

He looked inside, found the cable that connected me to all that was toxic, temporary and elegantly unplugged, connecting me to the socket where the electricity of love ran constantly. Somehow, he always knew which switch to keep on.

Future.

You asked me if I could turn the clouds pink, I know it's
something you wanted but I couldn't change the world.
You said *love looks beautiful in grey* I didn't know what you
meant or understood how grey- a colour of desolation could
amount to love, such a wholesome thing.
I even remember the smile on your face when you wrote the
last word to a poem, it was all you needed.
But time, time is what you don't want, but need.
This changes everything, because with time I now understand
why I thought love looked beautiful in grey, and now I look at
the pink clouds every morning and I longer smile at my last
word of a poem but feel fulfilled at every word.
You have these grey eyes to give you strength, you can change
the world, after all you made the clouds turn pink.
What's next?

Patience

There is this curled creation that exists as the initiation to the
montage of our lives.
 A slight curl that begins my name and an upside-down
exclamation mark that belongs lost in the third position to my
name.
 I present to you the one and only- question mark.
A pen crafted,
mouth moulding and heart tearing decor to every lifeline.
 The standard 'do you love me?'
A delicacy of a melody that screams a silent uncertainty.
 To the 'how could you?'
Less of a question more of an underlying declare that whispers
anger.
 This curled creation shatters,
heals and controls but have you ever placed an inverted
question mark next to a normal question mark?
 Does it look like a heart?
Does it look whole?
Perhaps this is your answer,
the uncertainty of a question mark lives its life not whole but
halved,
just like you always know half of every story until both question
marks can speak-both partners can speak, and both question
marks can create the whole heart of what is, your love.

Echoing lives

The truth is some people are too complex to be happy.
They need to know the works, the blueprints of its formation,
the roots of the world. They need to understand why they feel
what they do, they need to see what is written about, never
seen but always illustrated.
They need to understand the worlds beginning in order to
understand themselves. And the truth simply is the world is
famous for its theory's, debates and war.
But whether the truth has been found it is too complexly
hidden within the sand of
debates and contradictions to be truly detected.
And this human complexity is what restricts us from happiness.
From the truth of acceptance- that we are alive but live to find
out why.

Belated love

She is no diamond, no angel-no flower.
In fact, she is nothing that's typically associated with beauty
and innocence.
She is that broken glass table at the second-hand store.
She's that beautiful lamp on your nightstand you always forget
to place batteries in.
But you just don't understand one thing.
One day you'll move out,
 and that lamp you left behind will someday be owned by
someone who will always keep it glowing,
And it'll light up the entire room like a thousand stars.
It's beauty, a sparkle from the window of another's heart and in
that very moment, you'll feel like an empty lamp-wishing you'd
just cared a little bit more.

One life

You hate rain because it makes you cold,
adore baths because they bring comfort
and love the ocean because it brings you freedom.
But all that gives you freedom and comfort is made of the same
thing that brings you cold pain.
The world is one existence,
and everything it is becomes everything we are, by choice.
You choose whether to like or dislike, but make the choice to
condition yourself to love the pain,
 because it's the thing that keeps happiness as a birthday party
surprise you dread, but end up loving the memory of, maybe
not now, but for a lifetime.

You have no choice

Stand.
You can't sit around forever and slowly drown in your pain,
because time won't stop for you, for anyone.
You can't cry for weeks and expect someone to knock on your
door and heal you, because most of the time that pain is self-
designed,
so how do you expect someone else to know the remedy to your
architecture?
You can't fear love and hope that it'll find you with an open
heart because real love is commitment and sacrifice,
you can't expect an open heart to pull yours in, when its locked.
You can't dream of success and expect your awakening to be
the replica of a dream. You can't give happiness just one smile,
 pain your time and hope that life will give you better.
Because if you fall, you have no choice but to stand again and
claim your power.

How love feels

For us the night the sky is an immeasurable black diamond.
Subtle sparkles on its edges named stars.
Of course, diamond is hard to break,
 but within this black diamond lives a world that cannot be
seen-through its window tint.
So dark you cannot see inside unless you are familiar enough
with the sky to ask at
which conditions our diamond can break?
But only we are.
Though our love lives through the night sky,
 it breaks this diamond every once in a while, to show this life
that our love owns its universe.
The world echoes our love in the silence of the night, it's depth
can be felt and its
volume can be heard.
The ground we walk upon cherishes our every step,
even oxygen feels privileged to have us breathe its existence.
The entire world has fallen in love with us.
Just wait for the night and it'll all come like an unexpected
raindrop.
Only we know how to enter this diamond, because we made it.
You'd think someone as young as us hardly knows much,
but we know enough to create an entire love, and ours just
happened to take the form of, a night sky.

To build and repair

There is damage within us all that equates to the scratch upon a glass window,
 a crack or a stain.
But the secret to this truth is that we need to understand which one it is.
If it is a stain, we just need to find the right solution to clean it, a scratch needs more than that, it needs patience and acceptance.
 The patience to be careful with how we handle our lives yet accept that pain is the beauty of growth.
A crack is a little bit different,
a crack within us requires not our entire replacement but the replacement of a bandage- what holds our life together.
What keeps us happy and fulfilled- when we find a crack, we need to replace the glue, before everything falls apart.

Owning success

The worst mistake you can make is ruining something you can grip within your palms,
for something you wish to grip with your entire mind.
A small amount of anything can outgrow the size of your palms, but holding
something as large as that, can no longer grow.
You're stuck with a creation that hasn't even grown from your own dedication.
Let your success be your own and your admiration- theirs.

My resignation

I have resigned way too early from the life that would have
come to me, far too late.
I have signed and dated every document there is in return for,
a guarantee that I'm free but if I have to sign my way into
freedom, is that letting this life go?
I've learnt young that the harder you pull a knot hoping it'll
undo the tighter it becomes and well, for a while my minds
been a knotted ball of- a timed cataclysm.
 I resign.
I am resigning from the job of people paying me to untie their
laced pain from
someone else's heart.
 I am resigning from living in a home built from bricks of my
clustered anxiety, carpet
made from irritable anger and lights made to distract me with
its artificial glow away
from the natural sunlight my soul could resonate with.
I resign from travelling to the depths of my past because every
time I return, I have to
somehow pay my future the debt of, priceless time.
 I'm resigning from the life that's kept me in a prison of my own
strength, words, pages
and documents that sum up what I thought I was made for.
To live shouldn't be today I sign that I am going to remain in
this home forever,

but that the only signature I should give is the one that lets me be free in growths hands.

I'm resigning, because well- I have found my own life within the home, love and future that's grown and built to be happy, strong and free of anyone who could knot my mind to a lamppost of signed- time.

Any more questions?

How do you know who to call when the world collapses in front
of you,
like a waterfall?
And the clouds leave, removing any sense of mystery from the
sky's proposal of life.
Will I take life to be mine, until death do us part?
How do we know what to believe?
Near the seasons that are untameable, running like cheetahs
across our lenses, we can't blink to restore a moment.
There, right there how do we know what time even is?
But above or beyond, to forever or finitely,
when our images of words and expectations of moments,
in video become distorted or broken,
 we don't understand that a second is an individual second.
Our whole life flashes with sirens before us.
How could I ever know life's story?
To question what or who you are among this living planet, gives
you only one response; the answer is never there, it is never
shaped in a form you've seen before and it is

never known until...

Unknown length, date or time; Welcome back.
You did it.
Look carefully ahead.
Yes.

It is there.
Yes really, that is it.
Now,
any more questions?

The fall of a leaf.

It becomes so lost in the journey down that it forgets its
landing- the end,
drifting towards the calls of wind, the last known moment of its
happiness,
but then,
it falls onto a table in a nearby garden, maybe a little child picks
it up and paints it or scrapbooks it,
Or it falls into the hands of a couple, a leaf has become their
souvenir of love, so they decorate their home with plants and
nature,
spreading the beauty of life to everyone, everywhere.
The leaf fell from the tree as if that was the end.
But it's fall lead to the rise of happiness the uplifting of
someone's world.
Forget the ending to this moment, lose yourself in the journey.

Galaxy rose

Sometimes we enclose ourselves like roses.
Petals and petals, walls and walls of everything we could be,
everything we could have felt.
Living in the very centre of this rose monument.
And these petals are orbiting around us like a galaxy, because
you are the universe. The very first petals are small in number
and size, but this petal of a planet is the closest to you, a planet
with rules of restriction to thought, feeling and creation.
The further out, the planets increase in all measures, and there
is no limit to human experience, but you're so far away that
when you look at them, you see no difference between the
petals right next to you and the world.
How heart-breaking that you live so enclosed by your fears, you
no longer recognise that happiness, that freedom exists.

Read carefully,
You are a universe, you have only lived in the centre of a rose.
You are not part of the petals or centre, you have only ever lived
there.
Let's travel to another planet of your dreams and wishes,
because to travel there doesn't require a rocket.
Only one wish and an indivisible mind.
You are the universe of your life,
what do you have to fear?

Passion or work?

I found myself in the vivid panorama of choice and my camera, the decision.

A mere capsule of medical recollection but prescribed by my picturesque views- no doctor.

No professional assistance, no qualified indentations.

No graded love.

No experienced masters in taking care of the blooming agriculture of my mind.

In fact, how could I take the picture when the button of imprisonment sees my views as a victim and not a culprit?

The lenses overdosed on these capsules- dizzy at the site of freedom, at the site of decision.

What do I do?

Once the camera shoots the decision is made, my views will remain pictures of

mountains of medicine but what if I can never smudge the ink to create a smudge resembling tropical literature?

What if my fingertips leave fingerprints of indecision on a picture painted by camera cartridge and not pen ink?

What if my vivid panorama of choice isn't a panorama but a square snapshot of my penned medicine, my writing and all I needed to do was press shoot? This will be a beautiful picture stained in- poetry.

I chose my passion.

The surface of a city

In a city of your awareness.
The seasons of your emotions don't shift their annual order,
and the buildings of your decisions don't re-mould into your
latest choice.
The businesses of your relationships do not grow or become
insolvent,
just because you lost control and time.
The world doesn't adjust to your lifeline.
Life is just a surface.
So,
Paint, artistical or not practice your dream on a continuous
recall.
Your surface, your canvas.
Solve, mathematical or not discover the method of your
greatest problem and find the answer. Your surface, your
notepad.
Prove, scientific of not give yourself a hypothesis of everything
you want to be and conduct as many experiments until your life
correlates positively with your mind. Your surface, your lab.
Write, poetic or not describe the world with a million emotions
and write as if you belong in the meaning of the most legendary
words.
Your surface, your novel.
Imagine holding a surface to look within and discover that life
is just the surface of a million layers of opportunity.
Your surface, your own design.

Ice cold or never told?

Don't freeze, even if your heart doesn't feel at ease,
time doesn't give you the ability to pause,
because freezing even for a moment breaks life's law.
You weren't made to stay in life afraid,
Or broken because you let your heart bleed out,
to quench the thirst of their soul which is in drought,
You weren't kept here to walk into a maze,
to pay the bills, please life with thrills, or live pointlessly just to
amaze. You weren't saved countless times from your ending to
live on the setting- I'm pending, moments you didn't even
know were your last,
because your protector gave you life again, so fast.
Don't freeze.
Your life is not a breeze but, it is more than you'd ever have
known could heal,
and more than you could have ever known could grow,
 and blossom into a garden, no, a forest of endless pathways if
you just keep walking,
and never freeze.

Beyond love

There are medications that cure one thing and harm another,
or heart transplants- sometimes something has to die in order
for another to live.
There is always deceit in all that will heal.
But loving you is nothing like this.
It is like laying my heart in only silk sheets having no idea that
a graphene love is
underneath, you're holding it.
It's like stepping onto a frozen lake with no idea how long it's
been frozen for,
but I step, I run across it because if I fall you've taught me that
swimming through pain is the only option.
It's like watching sunlight from my window in winter, stepping
out with thin clothing expecting it to be warm but I will come
outside, because facing what is meant to freeze
my happiness is the only way the struggle will melt.
In all that will heal there is deceit,
but this is why your love has always taught me how to live
through the healing process at no sacrifice, how to heal myself.
I would say you are like heaven-but you are far beyond.

Over thinking,

Do you over think or think over and beyond the bus stop of the happiness that
you could have felt?
Like driving past your destination over and over and over.
But soon,
 your car will run out of fuel so what if it stops in between joy and pain,
 What will happen then?
 Will you be happy?
Or hurt now because you're in limbo, as you watch the world pass you by.
 Let me tell you something.
 Everything ends,
but right now,
if you're able to breathe, to feel and to smile without... then you're alive,
for how long?
I don't know,
 but for now, yes.
Stop, stop ruining life with empty thoughts.

Silence -a winner

I speak this silence through empty eyes and solidly built smiles
Brittle.
You whisper the millionaire words rich from birth.
Malleable.
Your words spiral into every possible posture at which your
minds comfort rests.
Yet silence is your frangible discomfort,
a bowl filled with only whatever is left of you.
And when that bowl dives into the puddles of spoken
mendacity it breaks.
Brittle.
But condolences to words that could only get injured.
Malleable.
My broken pieces can be repaired in one direct way to fit their
position exactly right
my silence can be rehabilitated and enunciated in one straight
way,
but your words are sound waves formed from elasticity.
Silence is the winner.
Allow it, allow him, her, them and us to mould words into a
sculpture that silence
takes the form of.
Honesty.

Lust vs love

Just like liquid,
making up a high percentage of my body,
you,
wash away my apprehension,
sterilize my intellect and disinfect my perception - but liquid is
a category and you're not water.
Although you polish my exterior with your endearment,
you vandalize my interior organs with your inhumanity and
ruthlessness.
So yes, you're nothing like water but rather, like- bleach.

Heart or brain

It's not a war, nor a contradiction or a battle.
It's a pointless fight.
It's like punching that metal table leg you hit your foot on.
You're only hurting yourself by fighting it.
When a person who's never felt pain is asked what pain feels
like, they'll tell you what they have heard and what they've
seen, but not what they feel.
An emotionless and narrow, definition.
But when you place that question in the hands of one who's felt
pain,
they'll tell you what they know, what they have heard, what
they've seen and what they've felt.
An endless, extended and real experience.
Who do you trust more?
Who do you follow?
The person who's felt the pain, right?
Then why is it called a battle between the heart and the brain.
You've chosen yours.
It's not a war, nor a contradiction or a battle.
It's a pointless fight.

Living cell

You say you're in prison
And the worst thing is you're not in prison
Your free but handcuffed to tragedy
Your sentence isn't served in between walls,
it's in broken air, your freedom broken and your soul bare
Yes, today the world is more understanding
But we're all still falling with no landing
I'm buried alive,
she's digging and you're drowning.
And happiness is a construction site no one is founding.
We all float, we all drown or suffocate,
because nothing is easy to generate.
But here's the unscientific or evidenced truth,
your mental health can die while your body survives,
give your mind the same extent of luxury, necessities and
components as you give to your body.
And no.
Not just for survival, but enough to live or feel alive.
I understand it's never easy,
just enjoy the last moments.
And with everything you speak, give it permission to colour in
your world.

Universal distance

Distance breathes the air trapped between unspoken words,
unseen faces, unknown pains.
It nourishes itself from plates of served pride and wishes to
drink the little vulnerabilities we possess.
Distance finds the cracks and heightens the appearance, but it
also sees the decor of love upon a face,
music within a voice and the familiarity of a homely face,
then heightens it too.
It seems as though its nor an enemy or friend but a
programmed system
with one rule-to play fair.

Misunderstood mentality

In a bathtub filled with your favourite bath soak,
 you seem to see bubbles that are formed from a simple
composition of chemicals your bare skin touches.
In a bathtub filled with bath soak I see bubbles of oxygen that
have accidentally been pushed of the edge,
caught on the rock of your foot drowning at the bottom of your
bathtub,
then you allow the slow release to the point where they surface
as foam on
the surface of water, the surface of your mind.
I see the layers of bubble as a layer of protection for oxygen, to
protect it from your
impulsive touch.
This is why I am misunderstood,
 because when you see a diver underwater for longer than its
tank supplies oxygen, you see him suffocating.
I see him losing his life to repay oxygen because he didn't listen
to its rules.
He didn't understand life's limitations- surviving the human
mind when flooded with bleakness.
 It's about time, we force oxygen to surrender to our survival,
now attempt
to inhale when we surrender to oxygen.
Surrender the life within our minds to either -satisfaction and
peace or,
regret and

futility.

Save me?

Remember when hell is within, heaven-you are without.
When will you understand, you set fire to your own skin
screeching in terrorising pain,
imploring something, anything to stop the pain?
 But when will you understand God isn't in charge of the
underworld,
 who are you asking in that mirror?
You set fire to your own skin and heart, yet you are the only fire
fighter your eternity has ever seen.
When will you understand that with every eternal breath you
take,
you choose whether the oxygen within will live to light the fire
of hell or extinguish the flames that could turn your heaven
into-ash?
Turn you into ash.
The only saviour to a humanity of heaven and hell is yourself.
When, when will you understand that as long as you're
breathing, you live
through both?

Ocean blue

Shards of nirvana, mellow at your footsteps,
depths of liquid compassion, dulcet with your aches and most
importantly floatation,
a minds liberation tracing with no indentation, medicinal, a
skins natural healer.
Here lay sixteen shades of ocean blue. Him.
The trepidation of a navy ocean survives on the formulation of
oxygen. It swims on the traces of your skin. Dive and the navy
ocean's heightened turbulence becomes a tranquillity-soaked
paradise. A storm of navy blue is a storm of wrapping paper.
The tropical finish of turquoise lingers in the Maldivian sea,
cascading with two thousand species, two thousand drops of
the world's-soaked paradise.
Overhead were the royal blue yachts, who's passengers if
worthy to dive into the two thousand species, would fall in love
with serene blue, their eyes dripping with
the liquid door to this aquatic heaven, forever clueless. Forever
surfaced with shallow
captivation, an imprisonment of dreams. The remaining
passengers always drifted on
impressions of a beautiful depth of this ocean. The beautiful
depth of his mind.
Arctic blue, the home to a temporarily iced princess, the queen
of an entire arctic

ocean- my dearest snow. Sprinkled over the stellar white coat of a polar bear, rested her reflection. The only constellation of the ocean's and sky's depth in a human physique.

Our dearest snow. Arctic blue. Our arctic fairy-tale. Lastly starfish blue, a map of destinations. Five hopes, five formulations that will

begin with a forever 'I adore you'.

Navy, turquoise, royal, arctic and starfish blue. All will manifest the one phrase that has come from your eyes and my heart when you told me.

"I adore you".

Hearts freedom

Don't hold onto hate.
Don't keep that ball of anger bowling down the alley of your happiness.
They hurt you, they gave you the bowling ball, and the hurt they caused you will heal, but the hurt your causing yourself by holding onto that hate won't.
Put the ball down, before your heart's pins collapse.

Reversible existence

Your eyes will burn and everything you have ever seen,
condenses into a few ashes,
 into dust.
Everything you have ever been disappears into the silence
oxygen holds prisoner.
A prisoner we are so desperate to breathe until it takes us back.
And even the stains on humanity, ink marks on paper,
buildings handcuffed into the cell of our ground.
Everything free or captured slowly corrodes, and silence
becomes our existence.
We are dust,
but we live as if we are concrete.
Devoting our powdered bodies to systematic routine,
until we fall onto the concrete of our egotistical deception and
realise dust belongs amongst freedom, air and dislocation.
But by then our oxygen would have expired,
 we do become dust,
but rather as dead skin cells,
and not the fairy dust we once could have been.

Expire

Everything comes with an expiration label,
so that you know by which date to consume anything edible,
but you see with everything else,
it's not that we can't see the label but it's one of two things;

We forget that things expire,
or we continue to consume things that are out of date with our
lives,

and both of those things will destroy you internally or
externally.

Despair

You raise hell fire, just to burn your way out,
you detain your soul within sand just to feel your heart in
drought.
You are so numb that you cannot feel so you force yourself to
heal,
from a disease where nothing around you feels real,
you dedicate your life to pharmacy,
creating powerful medications that amplifies your serotonin in
secrecy,
and you become your own lawyer, incriminating yourself for
every crime you committed against your success,
and you find yourself destroying the ecosystem of who you are,
throwing plastic in the rivers of your pain, ceaselessly.
You destroy yourself with every wrong move.

Life

You've given me the most ethereal gift in the world- the
cleansing of my stained eyes, restoring what was once my view
of a world covered in disinfectant-serenity.
 Before I met you every morning the window view was
decorated in fog,
no matter how hard I tried to blow away, clean, spay the fog- it
never went.
It was as if I was trying to see a world that didn't exist- until I
met you.
A world where pain was healed, happiness was intense, and
love was infinite.
That morning when I awoke,
for the first time in my entire life the window view was sterile,
an outline of each particle of life clearly distinguishable.
For the first time I looked to see, listened to hear and felt to
understand- all because your love was real, so life had to be.
I finally understood what life was, why we need love.
Opening the window, for the first time I felt my lungs satisfied.
The sun was so delighted that it could sparkle, it broke through
the glass and
embraced my entire body. That morning suddenly the floor was
no longer cold wood, it was the softest carpet my feet have ever
touched, gifting me with the freedom to walk upon the ground
for as long as I desired to feel life.
The bathroom mirror was no longer blurred, I saw myself for
the first time, grey eyes

as strong as steel and with your brown -the beauty of sunlight and gold's value

nothing could break life's purpose.

You gave my lungs a new routine, to breathe and oxygenate my mind until they were

satisfied.

To live my life as if every particle I respire is limited.

You are love.

Love cleans even the cloudiest view to see that a life will always have purpose, regardless of how foggy it may appear.

And this is what our life is; a body with an instruction manual for survival, whilst you learn to turn that manual into a book that gives every breath- serenity, every

movement-intensity and every view-emotion. And with love by your side, each of those experiences are crystal clear.

Imitation

Everything you knew isn't real.
Reality is our worlds limit.
Independence and relationships co-exist,
as a reoccurring error when typed into life at once.
Because the truth aches but fantasy breaks.
And maybe relationships were always about comfort,
 and independence was about the denial of a need we package,
never open but admire.
Expectations are not real,
they are rules generalised from how some people feel.
Time doesn't exist as we know it,
 it's an illusion to measure and systemise our lives.
And our lives may not be real because,
 if heaven exists this is a game we have to win.
Nothing is real except your soul,
with separation as a deceiving dimension,
the more you feel, see or hear it,
the less meaning and passion it will withhold.
forget the world's control and system, and live in a way that
awakens your soul.

Tragic

Everyone is born for themselves.
Not to accomplish but to complete,
Not to create but to delete.
Not to conquer but just to defeat.
It's a tragedy, a shipwreck of identity.
We clash against the waves of everything we want to be and
instead of the ocean healing us, it destroys,
but every drop creates this ocean, so is it really our fault?
You damage for someone else to fix,
and they ignore for someone else to see,
the damage is left cracked or bleeding and the world becomes
cracked and bleeding.
we watch it bleed staring like our hearts do not know how to
help,
 because the ambulances of our humanity have stopped, a flat
tyre punctured by our selfishness.
None of us call for help, but the hospitals are,
empty.

Time passing

You are promised a life as long as the ocean line,
 but no one warns you about the quicksand of- time.
You think you are paralysed in between the feeling of living in
this moment
or preparing for the future of life's tournament.
You work to build a life that satisfies all but yourself,
to find that each lifetime moulds into a shelf,
displaying everything you made here.
What have you made?
I guess you are the sculptor, with a time limit.
I guess you are a traveller, with finite fuel.
But most importantly you are not paralysed between life and
death, you are free because you can choose how to spend every
breath.

As long as you're breathing, this life is your power.

And everything you breathe, let it become everything you could ever be.

Oxygen is yours, so own it.

Printed in Great Britain
by Amazon

72844066R00139